GRATITUDE: A WORK IN PROGRESS

GRATITUDE: A WORK IN PROGRESS

BY AUSTEN BROWER

NEW DEGREE PRESS

GRATITUDE: A WORK IN PROGRESS

ISBN   978-1-63676-729-1 *Paperback*
         978-1-63730-038-1 *Kindle Ebook*
         978-1-63730-140-1 *Ebook*

Table of Contents

———

To my family, a book written by a Brower.

Wear gratitude like a cloak, and it will feed every corner of your life.

RUMI

gratitude:

———

The Hallmark thank you card, Sally, stood at attention on a coffee table prepared for her life's mission. She was a small two-and-a-half-by-four-inch card, slightly textured with a bold blue "Thank You" centered on a field of white and fenced in by two blue lines. The pen, her commander in arms, was a simple blue and clear BIC that relaxed nearby. This "thank you" note was from an incredibly historic lineage. Sally's ancestors are from the ancient Chinese and Egyptian empires that once ruled the world, although they were slightly different, composed on papyrus and written as reminders of friendship or good luck notes. By way of Europe, Sally's ancestors immigrated to the US. "In 1856, Louis Prang, a German immigrant, brought greeting cards and notes to America." As a Hallmark card, Sally was born in Lawrence, Kansas, at a production center. She departed for a department store and then landed on Austen's desk in Washington DC.[1]

Sally drifted between waking and sleeping for who knows how long until her day finally came. Taken up

———

1 Bernie Seter, "Thanksgiving And Thank You Notes," *Northern Crossing* (blog), November 24, 2018.

by the sender, she left the confines of the box, vaulted into the world quickly, coming to rest on a desk. Sally stretched out for the first time since she was closed, which revealed a blank canvas. To that day, she had wondered what gratitude she would fulfill. As her sender, Austen, started to write using the silent but focused BIC pen, Sally learned her purpose.

Austen had been a barista at La Colombe Chinatown DC next to Capital One Arena, where the Capitals hockey team played. He often conversed with guests as he took their orders and made drinks. On one particular evening, he crafted two lattes: one for a gentleman with a Capitals hockey lapel pin on his strapping suit and the other for the man's son. The guests sipped their lattes in peace. Upon leaving, the gentleman in the strapping suit offered Austen two tickets to the Caps game. To Austen's surprise, he later watched the game five rows back from the ice behind the goal! The man with the lapel, Dr.Holtby, was more than a fan of the Washington Capitals—he was the team dentist. Months later, on July 16, Sally became Austen's 172 "thank you" card of the year. He said, "This note is long overdue, but know your kindness has resonated through my life. I have told many about your gesture!" Family, friends, and acquaintances heard the story of Dr.Holtby. Kindness and gratitude spread each time.

To send Sally, Austen had donned and sealed her envelop. Address, postage, and return address (hopefully never to be used) were the final touches before she entered the United States Postal Service. Ben Franklin was the first Postmaster General in 1775. The system's purpose was to "bind together the scatter populous of the new United States." The organization grew to employ over

633,000 employees, making it the third-largest civilian employer. Over one hundred and eighty-one million pieces of first-class mail are processed and delivered daily. With a giant organization servicing all the United States, it was no wonder the trepidation Sally felt entering the blue drop box on the corner of Colombia and Ontario RD NW. Though she was afraid, understanding her mission was vital to continue the chain of gratitude started with Dr.Holtby. She was ready. Over the next few days, she journeyed by van, was sorted by hand due to her square shape, returned to a van for transportation, and delivered by the good people of the US Postal Service, fulfilling her destiny![2]

Besides being cute, Sally's journey explains the odyssey "thank you" notes survive to arrive at their destinations. Throughout 2020–2021, I sent over 365 messages similar to Sally to family, friends, acquaintances, and strangers. My notes have traveled from DC to California, Ohio, and even the United Kingdom. The greeting card industry's infrastructure and interoperability, postal system, and history behind them are all astounding. Before starting our journey together, I wanted to highlight the trip many "thank you" notes take to bring simple gratitude to their recipients.

---

2 Boyce Upholt, "The Tumultuous History of the U.S. Postal Service—and its Constant Fight for Survival,"*National Geographic,*May 18, 2020.

.00

a journey

———

Grey weather settled over Washington, DC, as 2020 began. A year that would cause societal isolation started with many social gatherings. People were expected to hibernate in the winter. However, there was no time for resting as an MBA student. My girlfriend in San Diego and a flexible schedule left me to my own devices. Every weekend and many weeknights, my classmates and I partied. Hangovers were the outcome of that formula. I was disappointed in my productivity and lonely the mornings after. A busy school schedule and social media could not keep the loneliness away. Partying was fun and not always a harmful activity, but deep down, I knew most good things didn't leave someone wallowing in self-pity. Nursing a hangover one morning, I thought, "Things must change."

Gratitude was the first thought that came to my mind. It would require me to reflect on positive elements of my life. Maybe I was a suck-up, but even as a kid, my parents' friends would compliment me on my "thank yous." But how to ritualize it? Before getting too far into brainstorming a solution, I brewed coffee. My days started with coffee, reading, and reflection. That morning, as I racked my brain for an answer, I drank deeply. My ritualized mornings were something I already did. I thought instead of creating a whole new "self-improvement" ritual, what if I added something to my morning one?

Drinking coffee and watching the sunrise reminded me of my dad. I observed him sipping coffee while writing "thank you" notes to family, friends, strangers, and business associates at an early age. The paper's crisp lines, embossed letters, and his aggressively slanted handwriting prompted me to touch and admire the notes. The purpose of my dad's messages were to maintain and develop relationships. Together, we would drop them at the post office and, on occasion, pick up donuts from a local shop. Remembering the "why" behind his notes, I decided to ritualize gratitude by sending "thank yous."

My goal was to write a "thank you" note a day for a year. I believed I could push myself to be more self-aware and have an eye toward celebrating others in everything I did. The objective of my "thank yous" was to share positivity and strengthen relationships in my life and community. I had no clue what was in store. Days turned into months. The consistent act started to transform me. Relationships deepened, and my loneliness abated. I gave gratitude more willingly. My community grew. At the same time, sending notes seemed very simple, accessible, and sometimes insignificant. I wondered if my feelings and project were unique or part of a larger trend today— what I found changed the way I saw simple gratitude.

Today, we connect more than ever through a wide range of digital media, including text, tweets, and emails.

Each day, the average internet user spends two hours and twenty-two minutes on social media, professionals receive about 120 emails, and Americans send around ninety-four text messages.[3] Despite all these easy ways to communicate, loneliness is a growing problem in the United States. Three in five Americans are lonely, "with more and more people reporting feeling like they are left out, poorly understood and lacking companionship," according to a report by Cigna, a health insurer.[4]

"Social media use alone is not a predictor of loneliness. In all the findings, a lack of meaningful human connectedness is paramount."[5] I do not believe social and digital media hold all the blame, but they encourage surface-level conversations and provide a quick, temporary, shallow fix to deeper, personal needs. Social media makes it extremely easy to fire off a message of gratitude, hate, love, humor, and criticism. Often these messages do not have much forethought, depth, or effort in their development. Specifically, on gratitude, people have perceived that the appetite for it has declined when in reality, even with social media and texting, Americans are just worse at expressing it.[6] The world seems to be in a convoluted state where accessibility to people is high, but genuine relationships are challenging to develop and strengthen. My year-long gratitude practice

3 Denis Metev, "How Much Time Do People Spend on Social Media? [63+ Facts to Like, Share and Comment]," *Review42* (blog), November 21, 2020.

4 Elena Renken, "Most Americans Are Lonely, And Our Workplace Culture May Not Be Helping," *NPR*, January 23, 2020.

5 Frank J. Ninivaggi, "Loneliness: A New Epidemic in the USA," *Psychology Today* (blog), February 12, 20219.

6 Simon-Thomas and Smith, "How Grateful are Americans?" *Greater Good Magazine*, January 10, 2013.

and substantial research showed me that gratitude is the foundation of positive relationships.

Sara B. Algoe, a researcher at the University of North Carolina, tells us, "Gratitude is important for forming and maintaining the most important relationships of our lives, those with the people we interact with every day."[7] Her Find-Remind-Bind Theory of gratitude "posits that the positive emotion of gratitude serves the evolutionary function of strengthening a relationship with a responsive interaction partner."[8] Lisa A. Williams is a lecturer at the School of Psychology at UNSW Australia. Her take on "thank yous" and Sara B Algoe's research is "Saying 'thank you' goes beyond good manners. At the end of the day, initiating a social bond can be risky. We need to be selective and choose to invest in those bonds with the highest likelihood of being a good investment. In this context, an expression of gratitude serves as a signal that the expresser is a good candidate for a future social relationship."[9]

Even simple gratitude carries with it positive societal markers. Gratitude is doing more than we think, even if it can be easy to deploy. Moving away from the science, gratitude is on "fire." A quick search displays 558 books on gratitude, twenty-nine podcasts, endless articles, blogs, and gratitude journals. Gratitude has taken the world by storm. Even as the power of gratitude is on the rise and more communication tools than ever are

---

7 Sara B. Algoe, "Find, remind, and bind: The functions of gratitude in everyday relationships,"*Social and Personality Psychology Compass*6, no. 6 (2012): 455–469.

8 Ibid

9 Lisa A. Williams, "Why Saying 'Thank You' Makes A Difference," *Lifehacker*, September 7, 2014.

inexpensive and available, people still believe that genuine "thank yous" are difficult.[10] The paradox of gratitude, surprising research, mentors, and my own experiences with gratitude provoked me to write this book.

Writing a gratitude book was somewhat of an accident. I had written notes for months before being talked into it. I am incredibly grateful I was. Sending notes and writing the book allowed me to practice gratitude while researching and interviewing practitioners like Brian Doyle, Jo Englesson, Darin Hollingsworth, and Amit Kumar. Gratitude concepts were uncovered such as secondary "thank yous" and my five phases for building a gratitude ecosystem. In a secondary "thank you," the sender writes appreciation to a second-degree connection. As an example, I wrote to my college friend's parents who were just acquaintances. Sending consistent gratitude, I discovered fascinating effects on the relationships it touched and my perceptions of gratitude.

Gratitude requires vulnerability. As a man, sometimes societal and business norms dictate a certain amount of invulnerability. Initial attempts to share gratitude in highly masculine circumstances or publicly left me feeling raw. Early notes tomasculine figures in my life, such as my first boss, who is tall and suave, gave me an insecure feeling. The project's consistent nature forced me to push through discomfort by the sheer number of "thank yous." Receiving supportive feedback from recipients and friends, I soon overcame the emasculation feeling that society had thrust upon me at birth.

---

10 Kumar and Epley, "Undervaluing Gratitude: Expressers Misunderstand the Consequences of Showing Appreciation,"*Psychology Science*29, no 9 (June 27, 2018): 1423-1435.

My journey showed me that tangible, genuine gratitude is not difficult. The right mindset, infrastructure, and approach to gratitude can deliver consistent appreciation, compounding impact in one's life and others, while generating epicenters of extensive pro-social behavior. These components were the foundation of a framework for building a gratitude ecosystem. Luckily, this book project took place during my MBA program. MBAs learn many frameworks pertaining to marketing, supply chains, decision-making, and leadership. The list continues, but you have to get an MBA to learn our secrets. Taking inspiration from my courses, I started to categorize and simplify my actions into an overarching framework—a five-phase gratitude framework. Unsurprisingly, the framework consisted of five steps. These steps helped me think about and then do the gratitude project.

1. **Set the Mindset** - Declare a "why" and manage expectations.

2. **Tie to Talents** - Design a project based on personal skills.

3. **Identify stakeholders** - Determine possible recipients of gratitude.

4. **Prepare & Simplify Deployment** - Clear potential barriers to success.

5. **Reflect & Celebrate** - Contemplate and share the experience.

I have spent a lot of my time in the business or education world. Therefore, after I constructed the five phases, I considered how they could apply within alternative contexts. There is ample evidence that gratitude improves business and learning outcomes. I believe that my framework can make substantial improvements within both. Though not the book's primary focus, I hope it leads to a more universal adoption of gratitude.

A simple "thank you" can be ritualized, resulting in transformative moments for senders, receivers, and the people around them. By building the infrastructure for quick accessibility to gratitude and easy deployment, people can change their perspective of others, themselves, and the world. It is never too late or unwarranted to share gratitude. This book's stories, observations, and framework are for those curious about exploring their past and present relationships and brave enough to become vulnerable in expressing gratitude.

Even though the gratitude project helped me maintain a healthy mental state throughout the coronavirus pandemic, my intention was not to make this a self-help book. I am merely a student of gratitude who wanted to share stories from my journey and a few learnings. That being said, there are compelling reasons for practicing gratitude in difficult times. I believe that people will always need more gratitude in the present more than in the past. We will explore stories of gratitude, research, 365-day grateful projects, and a simple five-phase framework within the book.

A gratitude project, like life, requires the persistence to show up every day, learn, and adapt. Life has no end-state or clear objectives besides death. Our human condition is to make progress and overcome constant setbacks. Like life, I have come to learn that gratitude has no end-state.

Gratitude requires one to choose it and act upon it every day. Some may even say it is always *a work in progress.*

Reader,

> *Thank you for choosing to read this book. I look forward to being your guide as you tour between the covers. My hope is that it inspires you and further connects you to the people in your life.*

A. BROWER

PART 1

.01

a community

———

Bill,

Thank you for the opportunity to work with you. You created a flexible environment where I could learn, grow, and hopefully help out the company. The further I get into the MBA, the more I appreciate the experience with you. Thank you for your kindness and support since.

A. BROWER

Austen—

I wanted to thank you for the note that you mailed to me. While I'm a firm believer in culture being organic within companies, I also realize that it largely comes from the top down, and so I really appreciate your generous words. If I can be of any help, you know where to find me, and I'm certainly here as a reference if you ever need one.

Enjoy the weekend stay safe,

BILL

Out of college, I went to work for a research-based media company. My role was to make sixty-plus cold calls a day. Day in and out for months, I dialed C-suite and executive-level professionals. Hearing "no" became my daily ritual. My job was not fulfilling, so I regularly looked for ways to find fulfillment. Reading that gratitude was the means to become a more appreciative, live-in-the moment type of person, I thought I would give it a go. Gratitude journaling was one way to practice. So, I attempted to list three to five reasons I was grateful, every night, before bed. Hours of cold calls made my eyes droopy and mind slow by the evening. Writing a list of gratitude in bed usually resulted in me sleeping.

In short order, my attempt at gratitude journaling was not a success. Instead, the practice left me with multiple journals whose first few pages had lists of gratitudes. If someone had graded those journals, they would come out to a "D+" due to their repetitive nature, missed deadlines, and modest use of gratitude. I started only to show appreciation for my coffee. The journal was a failure, but not without its learnings. I learned valuable lessons on how my brain worked and what I needed to do a successful gratitude project.

1. *I liked reflecting on gratitude.* Delightful little things like coffee, the beautiful golden light of the morning, and the people in my life composed my daily list of gratitude.

2. *Expressing gratitude in a journal was too isolating.* Saying "thank you" to how the golden light coats red brick buildings in an armor of gold was evocative imagery, but the building never responded to me.

3. *Commitment to the project required ritualizing gratitude into my life.* I had failed at practicing gratitude consistently because I was unable to weave it into existing rituals.

These early lessons helped guide the structure of my 365-day gratitude project, but by no means was I a gratitude expert when the year-long project started. Like me, many others have participated in a year-long gratitude journey, including Brian Doyle, A.J. Jacobs, Hailey Bartholomew, Dan Brower, John Kralik, and Mr. Elsner. Their stories highlight that gratitude projects are attainable by everyday people. Each gratitude practitioner learned unique lessons. However, similar core elements compose their project: an origin event (rough weekend, lousy year, unhappiness, or even reading this book! Can't blame me for trying, eh?), length of time, method of gratitude, and tracking. Outside of liking their stories, these gratitude practitioners are interesting because they influenced different phases of my gratitude framework, which I dive into later in the book.

Brian Doyle

Brian Doyle's 365-Day Gratitude Project

- Origin event: Near-death collision

- Period: One Year

- Method: Phone call or coffee

- Metrics/Tracking: Publishing a blog

The first time I heard Brian Doyle's TEDxYouth talk was during a morning practice of reflection and gratitude. Brian grew up in sunny San Diego between the ocean and mountains. He swapped the sunny shores for low limestone buildings, hot, humid days, and the seat of western power—Washington, DC for college. Brian thrived in bustling DC. He majored in Human Services and Social Justice, played club sports, and socialized with peers. Home for the holidays on January 1, 2012, and ecstatic to be with friends, he and his crew drove carefree in the streets of San Diego. Out of the blue, a car careened towards them. Brian made a last-minute adjustment to their course to avoid the vehicular impact that would have forever changed his life direction.[11]

Stopped at the side of the road, his heart pounding, he remembered thinking, "Where did I stand with the relationships in my life...Did they know how I appreciated them?" Month after month, life on the outside continued as before. Classes, extracurriculars, dates, parties, and fun paraded past. On the inside, Brian said he "continued to think about all the unfinished conversations in life, all the phone calls I had ended without an 'I love you,' and all the loose ends I had with people I cared about."[12] The unsettling thought that family, friends, and mentors did not know their impact on him continued to churn internally until Thanksgiving eleven months later. Reflecting on the year and Thanksgiving triggered an idea to call one person a day, let them know why he appreciated them, and then publishing a blog about them.[13]

Conversations with his dad, friends, and characters in his life revealed to him that "People don't know we appreciate them unless we show it and verbalize it. We hope they do, think they know, we assume they know. They honestly just don't unless we tell them." Daily gratitude opened the door to a vulnerability different from the one that consumed him during the near-death incident. Expressions of appreciation opened his heart to others

11 *TEDxYouth,*"365 Days of Thank You: Brian Doyle," January 19, 2015, video, 8:35.

12 Ibid

13 Ibid

and strengthened his relational bonds. His project was simple: a phone call and blog post a day.[14] Conversations with Brian underscored how powerful his "why" for the project was. That "why" fueled his dedication to his journey and influenced the first phase of mine: Set the Mindset.

Hailey Bartholomew

Hailey Bartholomew's Gratitude Project

- Origin event: A low point in life

- Period: One year

- Method: Photography

- Metrics/Tracking: Photobook

Hailey Bartholomew, a gratitude journeywoman, a photographer, and a mother, stood in the middle of the TED stage in a green and blue patterned dress. She spoke with confidence, yet her movements were timid. A 365-day grateful project led her to the stage like so many of my fellow gratitude practitioners.

Often in the first world, our accumulation of material goods and relationships lead us to believe we should be appreciative and happy. Hailey, like many of us, noticed the inconsistency between her perceived wealth and expected happiness. Even with all the ingredients for a happy life, she was yet to find one. She sought help from a nun in 2008. "I think the secret to happiness is reflection and gratitude," the nun explained and then laid out

14 Ibid

a ten-day gratitude challenge. The challenge required Hailey to reflect on each day for ten minutes, finding authentic moments of gratitude—not only moments where gratitude was expected.[15]

Ten days of reflection and gratitude captured her imagination and slightly quenched a previously unidentified thirst. "It sparked something amazing within me because I started to see things I wouldn't otherwise have seen, and they weren't the things you think." The spark caught fire; Hailey chose to intertwine her love of photography with the nun's advice. In 2008, Hailey started a 365-day project taking a gratitude photo a day.[16]

Day by day, she captured moments, actions, and people that elicited gratitude. Noticing moments and diligently photographing them transformed her world. Inconsequential elements such as the color green and its "brilliant different shades" evolved into lightning rods of reflection. Even good fortunes like "money on the meter when you have no money in the wallet" warranted a picture. In time, previous "catastrophic" events like rainy days became blessings because it meant "I got to use my favorite umbrella."[17] Small realizations, like beautiful beetles, developed into seismic ones. As can happen after years of marriage and kids, Hailey felt disconnected from her spouse, an atypical romantic.

He did not buy flowers or take her on dates. The daily photo quota required her to watch, wait, and see in a new light. One morning, in the vigilant state, she saw her

15 *Tedx Talks,* "365 Grateful Project | Hailey Bartholomew | TEDxQUT,» September 2014, video, 12:04.

16 Ibid

17 Ibid

husband give her, over anyone else, the biggest piece of pie. Taking that photo, she realized he had given her the biggest piece for years. These gestures were his romantic touch which would have gone unnoticed if it had not been for the gratitude journey. On the TED stage, she reflected, "Probably the biggest thing I learnt was how my expectations on other people prevented me from appreciating them for who they really were."[18] Bartholomew's story exemplifies better than most my second phase: Tie gratitude projects to talents.

A.J. Jacobs

A.J. Jacobs Coffee Project

- Origin event: Challenged by his son

- Length: As long as it took

- Way of gratitude: "Thank yous" to people in the coffee supply chain

- Metrics/Tracking: Thank every component of the coffee supply chain

A.J. Jacobs is a *New York Times* best-selling author, a journalist, dad, and gratitude journeyman who wrote *Thanks A Thousand.* Mr. Jacobs is an experiential author who likes to partake in adventures before writing his books. For example, living a year following a dogmatic reading of the Bible resulted in his book *The Year of Living Biblically.* Mr. Jacobs' son challenged him to thank every person within a food supply chain. As a guy who needs his coffee, Jacobs

---

18 Ibid

chose to thank people in the coffee supply chain—from bean to cup.

Even with coffee, A.J. is a self-proclaimed grumpy person; he wondered why and if gratitude could change the mood. By the end of his journey, he found answers to his questions. He discovered that the human brain is hardwired to see what is wrong in the environment to protect us from it. Therefore, humans naturally look to see what is incorrect in a situation; not what is going well. Gratitude trains the brain to emphasize the good things while still acknowledging the bad.[19] His project took him along what he dubbed a "Gratitude Trail" from Chung, his barista, to the coffee director of Joe's Coffee, a plastic cup designer, truck drivers, coffee farmers, and many more people in the chain.

His first "thank you" was to Chung, the barista. She, through stories, reminded him to look up and see people. "When dealing with people, I am going to take those two seconds and make eye contact because it reminds you, you are dealing with a human being."[20]Similarly to Brian Doyle, the journey generated unexpected conversations and many lessons. The key lessons he learned from gratitude are below and can be read about in his book or listened to on TED.[21]

- Look up.

- Smell the roses, the dirt, and the fertilizer.

---

19 AJ Jacobs, "A.J. Jacobs: My Journey to Thank All the People Responsible for my Morning Coffee," filmed June 2018,TED Salon: Brightline Initiative video, 15:21.

20 Ibid

21 Ibid

- Find who invented hidden masterpieces all around you.

- Fake it 'til you feel it.

- Practice six degrees of gratitude.

- Use gratitude as a spark to action.

The important thing for us to remember is that Jacobs was not a gratitude researcher or yogi. He was an ordinary person who became curious about the application of gratitude. This project took him around the world and changed his perspectives on himself, others, and coffee. He encourages people to follow their own gratitude trail, whether it is a sock, greeting card, or something else. In the end, he learned humans are naturally grumpy but have tools to change. Jacobs' choice to leverage a supply chain to identify his gratitude recipients influenced my thoughts on the third phase of my framework: Identify Stakeholders.

Dan Brower (My Dad)

Dan Brower's Gratitude Project

- Origin event: Business touchpoints

- Length: Life

- Way of gratitude: "Thank you" cards

- Metrics/Tracking: Relationships

Dan has been in the construction/building products industry for over forty-one years. He has consistently written "thank you" notes after sales calls, business

A COMMUNITY · 31

meetings, or in recognition of his employees. In his own words, "If you look at today, where basically it's emails and texts, and tweets and a lot of messages are down to 140 characters, I have found that when somebody actually receives something in the mail, it can be pretty powerful. They know there's been that additional time to write something and get a stamp and mail it to them, and they can physically open it up and read it."

Working in sales and account management required him to drive thousands of miles each year to client sites. He always had "thank you" notes and stamps stashed on the seat next to him, prepared to be used at a moment's notice. Following sales calls, lunches, or meetings, he would jot a quick note, stamp it, and take it to the post office. As he alluded to above, the extra steps he went to support a relationship were made easier for him by having the right supplies on hand. Notes have built strong business contacts, opened doors, and create genuine human connections. His recipients have responded in kind to his notes or even talk about them publicly. The positive feedback loop has therefore primed him to write more when the occasion arose.

Deployment of gratitude primes people to use gratitude more often, but gratitude is not the only objective. It's about furthering the relationship outside of the note, which requires time and intentionality. Dan brought the wisdom with his next comment: "[You] carry the message from the note all the way through your relationship." Notes or coffee chats are just another touchpoint. They are doors to further conversation and relationship development. To be primed for gratitude means leveraging all tools to foster healthy and more appreciative relationships. A phone call on a birthday or shared beers extends the note's intentionality. Touchpoints don't have to be planned in a gratitude project. My father, Dan Brower, is the one that taught me the art of "thank you notes" and is an excellent example of being primed for gratitude. Watching Dan helped me recognize the importance of Phase 4: Prepare & Simplify Deployment.

John Kralik

John Kralik's 365-day project

- Origin event: A low point in life

- Period: One Year

- Method: "Thank you" note

- Metrics/Tracking: Excel document with name, address, note

I learned of Mr. Kralik when researching this book. His audiobook took me a day to finish. (A great "read!") Mr. Kralik's professional career as a lawyer and personal life as a struggling divorced man and loving father hit a low spot in 2007. A potentially failing firm and recent breakup prompted an incredibly lonely trudge through the hills of LA.

While walking, he heard a voice. "Until you learn to be grateful for the things you have, you will not receive the things you want." The voice, along with a special note from his ex/maybe girlfriend, encouraged him to start a 365-day "thank you" project. Over the year, he would write a "thank you" note a day to family, friends, colleagues, customers who paid, and customers who did not.

The journey shifted his perspective, healed, and grew personal relationships with his sons, daughter, and girlfriend. It also reinvigorated the firm, causing customers to pay, and showed Mr. Kralik where to place his effort to get the most return. Daily gratitude changed how he perceived leadership and teamwork. It helped him ignore his pride, ask for help, and nominate a new partner to his firm.[22]

During the year, he had weeks where he didn't write a note. He had grace with himself, making up for missed messages at a later time. Gratitude projects don't mean life is sunshine and rainbows. There were times when excessive work and failed attempts at obtaining a judgeship almost brought him to new lows. The gratitude journey did reinvigorate relationships, which helped him get through these difficult situations. The journey resulted in 365 "thank yous," a marathon, and Governor Schwarzenegger's appointment to be a judge of the Los Angeles Superior Court. Once he started the project, Kralik took more time to reflect and celebrate his past, present, and future. Kralik's book and his stories solidified, in my mind, the importance of reflection and celebration—Phase 5 of my gratitude framework.

Mr. Elsner

Mr. Elsner's Project

- Origin event: Received one hundred birthday cards

- Period: As long as it took

---

22 John Kralik,*365 Thank Yous: The Year a Simple Act of Daily Gratitude Changed My Life*, read by John Kralik, London: Penguin eBooks, 2011, Audible audio ed., 5h 18m.

- Method: "Thank you" cards

- Metrics/Tracking: Respond to all his birthday wishes

Gratitude projects can also be impromptu. Mr. Elsner, a 102-year-old veteran, recently embarked on a gratitude project in response to birthday cards. Throughout his life, he was dedicated to gratitude and passed it onto his daughter. His daughter wanted his birthday to be special. She sent over one hundred blank birthday cards to people who knew Mr. Elsner with the hope that they write and mailed them to him. Elsner received over one hundred cards for his birthday. As a dedicated practitioner, and despite his hand arthritis, Mr. Elsner responded to all the birthday cards with "thank you" notes.

Elsner's project was simply a response to an outside trigger—one hundred birthday cards. It had a specific length, a method of gratitude, and metrics. I was lucky enough to get a call from Mr. Elsner. We talked about his family and what he had to do that day. Elsner was a regular guy. He did not have gratitude certifications or a special knack for saying thank you, besides perhaps his many years of experience. His story is an excellent reminder that these projects are diverse in their scope and approach. Gratitude projects don't require a degree or have to look a certain way. Most importantly, gratitude is still an effective means of acknowledging others no matter one's age.

Gratitude Projects Are For Everyone

Whether they are a singer, painter, writer, or musician, every artist gives themselves to their art. Songs, paintings, books, and symphonies carry their author's personality. The same can be said in any gratitude project or journey. The author of gratitude chooses the medium for expression—card, blog, or conversation. Each sign of appreciation carries the mark of the author. Gratitude's many forms are similar. However, five master painters could paint the same landscape resulting in five very different masterpieces. Though many of us have walked the path of gratitude, each path is a new journey of personal stories, changed lives, and a better world.

My friends would tell you that I was that guy who always had an activity or social event. When I was in the third grade, I taught myself to ride a unicycle. Junior year of high school, my mom and I started a high school model UN club. A few years back, I launched a coffee podcast (*Drip: A DC Coffee Podcast*—Free marketing?) because I wanted to learn the industry's stories. I loved diving into activities, industries, and ideas. Needing to reframe my focus on life, I turned to gratitude. Keeping the theme alive, I wanted to do more than just send a few "thank you" notes. Doing anything for a year seemed like an accomplishment, so I schemed to write 365 "thank you" notes in a year.

When explaining my journey to people, they often respond, "Wow! I could never do that [a 'thank you' note a day]." Brian Doyle would say, "My first recommendation is to not let the fear or the dauntingness of whatever your project is stop you from even starting." Gratitude projects are not uncharted waters. Many people have started and completed them. The stories above demonstrate that everyday people do them. Importantly, there is no wrong way to do a gratitude project, and one does not have to be an expert. Through the project I became quickly aware that I was not alone. Many people had, were, and will do year-long projects. I hope now there will be even more.

[**GRATITUDE OPPORTUNITY:** Write a "thank you" note to the author of your favorite song or book.]

.02

a few learnings

———

Dear Alice,

I remember visiting your house when I was growing up and listening to you train my mom. Your coaching and support gave her confidence to sing in some of the biggest concerts of the year. Because of you, my mom is a better singer, and I am a proud son. Thank you for being there for my mom. It was such a pleasure to get to know you over those years.

Best,

A. BROWER

Dear Austen,

I was so touched to receive your lovely note regarding my work with your mother on her signing. Your mother has always been more than a voice student with me. I count her as a true friend and have always loved to hear her sing in church.

ALICE

Austen Brower's "Thank You" Project

- Origin event: Emotional low point and yearning to reframe the mindset

- Length: 365 days

- Way of gratitude: "Thank you" note

- Metrics/Tracking: Excel spreadsheet

Growing up, my home bordered a creek. Traversing a steep raven was the only way to the water's edge. I would turn and repel down on my hands and knees. Once to the bottom, the sound of rolling waters and birds crept into my ears. Scents too hard to explain rushed to my nose while cool dampness rose to meet me. My siblings, friends, and trusty canine filled summers with building waterfalls, catching crawdads, skipping rocks, and walking the shores. Skipping stones was and is one of my favorite activities.

The best stones had soft surfaces and edges rounded by meandering waters. Nature designed smooth rocks for skipping. Like the water reshaped the stones, 365 days of gratitude has and continues to gently alter me. Every morning for a year, after brewing my coffee, I asked myself who I should send a "thank you" note to. The question prompted me to look back into time—days, months, and years. Friends who bought my puppy toys (#270), entrepreneurship class speakers (#68), my childhood friend (#167), and the apartment's trash collectors (#242) received notes. Waking every morning to that question, choosing a recipient, and deploying appreciation shifted my thinking bit by bit, morning by morning.

Life loves curveballs. 2020 brought the COVID-19 virus, the most disputed election in America's history, my grandfather's passing, and violent fires. My first response to these situations was anger and then sadness, but the story doesn't stop there. I can unequivocally say my gratitude project allowed me to recover faster and with more perspective and positivity than if I had not been doing it. I am still the same in many ways, but consistent gratitude changed how I joined into life, relationships, and conflict. My biggest takeaways reflecting on the 365-day gratitude project are an increased appetite for giving public gratitude and the tools to better mediated internal and external disputes. Like the skipping stone's impact on water, I have hoped my every act of gratitude caused ripples of appreciation.

Vocalizing Appreciation

Christina (#118, #247, #320) and I moved in together during a humid, pandemic-ridden summer. Each of us had roommates in the past and were used to each other, having traveled together from San Diego to Washington, DC, with a few stops in between. However, in the beginning, living together was a very new experience. We had beautiful days, but every once a while, tensions rose. She started to find it annoying that I left piles of books, headphones, and "thank you" notes throughout the apartment. In my defense, the piles were more like reminders for me to do something and looked like pristine, mini Eiffel towers. The numerous pillows I had to take off the bed to go to bed were substantial enough that a third person could have slept on the floor. Young in our relationships and living together, we had healthy interactions with a few tense conversations.

My gratitude project was in full bloom. Research continued with *The Gratitude Diaries* by Janice Kaplan. Kaplan catalogs how applying gratitude to her and her husband's relationship changed how they interacted, causing a reciprocal cycle.[23] Having given Christina many "thank you" notes by this time, I began to share my appreciation vocally. "Thank you for making our apartment a home," or when numerous skulls showed up, "Thank you for creating a fall atmosphere with the Dia De Los Muertos decorations." Vocalizing my appreciation had a reciprocal effect. She began to thank me more. "Thank you for doing the laundry today" or "Thank you for always putting the toilet seat down."

Vocalization had a few benefits. To vocalize, I had to acknowledge my appreciation publicly. Speaking appreciation felt different than writing it. It felt like I was putting myself on a ledge, waiting to see how she would respond. Christina always reacted kindly. By vocalizing gratitude for actions we appreciated, we positively signaled what we liked them to do. She liked when I helped out with chores, and I liked the environment she created for us. Expressing these feelings allowed us to build each other up in areas the other was already excelling. Appreciation gives us the power to highlight others' strengths and show that we value them and their contributions. The gratitude journey put me into a mindset where my first instinct was to thank.

Throughout the year of gratitude, unintentionally, I started to vocalize appreciation. Conversations with friends, colleagues, and strangers triggered statements of thanks. Living in gratitude made me much more comfortable to sit, reflect, and enjoy letting people know how impactful they were in my life. For example, my

---

23 Janice Kaplan,*The Gratitude Diaries: How a Year Looking on the Bright Side Can Transform Your Life*, read by Janice Kaplan, London: Penguin Publishing Group, 2015, Audible audio ed., 8h 12m.

good friend Rebecca (#199) sat on the phone with me for an hour, conversing on a few personal issues. Before the gratitude project, I would have said a surface-level thanks because delivering a real "thank you" would make me feel vulnerable and less masculine. Having the mindset of giving more genuine gratitude, I chose to comment, slightly uncomfortably, "Becks, thank you for being open about your experience, willing to listen to mine, and sharing insightful advice. Having a friend like you makes me feel heard and have a better understanding of how to navigate this experience." Repetition helped me overcome the feelings of vulnerability and emasculation.

Vocalizing gratitude in relationships seemed simple with friends and family. Before the project, displaying gratitude in the workplace was not so simple. As a young professional, I wanted to make my mark and show I could add value to the organization. Expressing gratitude for co-workers inherently meant I needed someone else to get something done. I fought feelings of inadequacy and social comparison. Therefore, sharing my gratitude for co-workers was difficult because it signaled to everyone that I needed help. My year of appreciation presented the opportunity to display gratitude publicly to co-workers. Many positive responses taught me not to withhold my gratitude in the workplace.

Working with teams in business school brought new lessons. Once I launched the gratitude project, almost every member of my various teams received a note of appreciation. Through the notes, I highlighted their contributions and value to the team, expressed my joy in working with them, and noted the project would not have been a success without them. Each note helped me to see every team member brought different strengths. The team was a micro-ecosystem of skills, personalities, and drive that coalesced to complete a project. Most team members responded with a kind text or comment reciprocating my value.

These particular interactions helped me realize:

1. Different experiences, skills, and personalities bring value to a group. My background was different but valuable.

2. Working on a team means that group members need something from each other to get a job done. One person cannot do it alone in a team or company.

3. Expressing gratitude creates a positive environment for people to fail, succeed, and learn—a.k.a. be accepted. It helps to mitigate jealousy and imposter syndrome. Someone else's success did not mean I was less successful.

Reflecting and practicing written appreciation on teams led to more public appreciation of teammates. During one team call for a social innovation class, we reviewed customer interviews. A teammate, Kirby (#46), had analyzed the conversations and presented the results for discussion. Her pre-work allowed the team to navigate the conversation deftly, resulting in a highly productive and fun meeting. I could not help myself. In the middle of it, I paused and said something like, "Wow, Kirby. Can we stop for a second? Thank you for doing all this. It is excellent and has made our conversation extremely productive." In true humble form, she deflected but later said thanks to the team on WhatsApp. The team continued to grow together, successfully submitting an "A" proposal.

A relatively shy person with praise, the gratitude project pushed me to share and relish the vulnerability that gratitude brought in front of others. My best managers always vocally appreciated my good work. It made me feel valued and like an essential part of the team. I didn't recognize it then, but gratitude solidified my loyalty to them and the team.

My consistent act of reflection and giving appreciation for 365 days started to blend into other areas of my life. Some of the most profound changes occurred as I became more comfortable vocalizing gratitude. Speaking gratitude created reciprocal relationships, strengthened friendships, and built trust in teams. Repetition helped me overcome vulnerability and emasculation previously felt during public expressions. Before the gratitude project, I felt shy expressing my gratitude. How will they take it? Will they think I want something? Do they think I am apologizing for something? A year of gratitude helped me become shameless in my appreciation.

Ability To Reframe

In September, Christina and I traveled to Portland, Maine, and Acadia National Park for a week. The shores, mountains, and wildlife of America's most northeastern reaches were incredible. With the beauty came a recognition of our privilege. We drove up from DC, stayed in hotels, camped, and drank local beers. Outside of sleeping on rocks and navigating Boston drivers, the trip was a superb opportunity to slow down, enjoy each other and our beautiful country. Returning to DC across the Memorial Bridge, the city's beauty struck me. That afternoon, Christina and I decided to take a bike ride to the Lincoln Monument and watch the sunset. The elevator lowered us three levels into the dark and echoing bows of the building's foundation to reach our bikes. My excitement for the bike ride plummeted with a quick look at my mutilated bike.

My bike's frame sat dejectedly, tilting forward onto its prongs. The front wheel had been stolen to complete a bike frame taken from the same rack. My heart sank, and my emotions felt like boiled lava within a porcelain vessel. I felt violated by an unseen stranger. Any gratitude I had felt for the day vacated my body. Anger, accusation, fear, and revenge coursed through me. In that instant, I believed people were evil and not to be trusted. I recognized the irony—a person doing a 365-day grateful project and writing a book on gratitude feeling so angry. So much for a gratitude project changing my perspective on life. Not until the next day did things change. I dropped my girlfriend off at the airport. The monotonous drive home lulled me into a thoughtful state. I recognized the tension I'd been feeling over the past few hours. Given some more time to think, the new habit of gratitude started to reassert itself.

Traveling at fifty-five miles per hour on a crisp fall day gave me a moment to clarify the previous day's events. I tried to reframe the negative experience. Instead of anger, I thought, "What can I be grateful for in the situation?" It dawned on me. I was grateful the thief didn't hurt anybody, including my girlfriend. Perhaps it wasn't the case, but I imagined the thief had to steal to put food on the table for their family. This train of thought caused me to feel appreciation for my lot in life. The incident and the moment of reflection helped me reaffirm my belief that people are inherently good. Even after the theft, Christina and I took a nice walk, still able to enjoy each other's company. Gratitude gives us the lens to reflect and rebuild broken or painful moments into more positive ones.

Dr. Emmons, the father of gratitude research, would not be surprised by my new skill to reframe. He wrote in *The Little Book Of Gratitude*, "When we respond to our lives, our past as well as events in the present, from a point of view of gratitude and appreciation, the way we interpret our experiences begins to shift and soften as we begin to soften inside."[24] Emmons goes on to explain that as a practitioner's "interpretation of life" expands and changes, "this capacity for existential resiliency and emotional flexibility in the face of an often disappointing reality is a hallmark for those who add the cultivation of gratitude...to their emotional repertoire."[25]

2020 was a year to remember. The civil division was surprising and can be characterized as a disappointing reality. The division started before 2020. A Pew Research Center study, based on a survey of five thousand adults, found "the divisions between Republicans and Democrats on fundamental political values—on government, race, immigration, national security, environmental protection, and other areas—reached record levels during

24 Dr. Robert A. Emmons, "The Little Book of Gratitude: Create a Life of Happiness and Wellbeing by Giving Thanks (London: Gaia Books, 2016), 45

25 Ibid

Barack Obama's presidency. In Donald Trump's first year as president, these gaps have grown even larger."[26] America has rocketed past civil discourse, a crucial tool in healthy democracies. Our polarization may deepen segregation within communities, undermine families, catalyze violence, decrease our health, and facilitate government gridlock.[27] To solve substantial issues while polarized is like trying to tie one's shoes while holding groceries in one hand and the dog in the other. (Don't ask how I know this.)

For over half my life, I have been a member of one political party. I even interned on the hill with one of the more extreme members during my college years. During the same undergraduate experience, I engaged with new perspectives, ideas, and people. Dating a first-generation American, working with openly gay classmates, and being beaten to a pulp by Locke, Rousseau, and Machiavelli kicked the hinges off my previously solidified beliefs. The confluence of new information drew me towards a different political identity like a magnet does to a nail. As a result, political discussions with family became lively debates. Even as my political identity shifted, I continued to vote with my family. Not until the 2016 election did I truly recognize my identity shift and vote for that identity.

2016 led to fascinating and even more heated debates. Politics were personalized. I am sure I am not alone in this. It was hard to separate candidates' actions from their supporters, many of whom were my family

---

26 "Political Polarization in the American Public," Pew Research Center, updated June 12, 2014.

27 Zaid Jilani, "What Is the True Cost of Polarization in America?"*Greater Good Magazine*, March 4, 2019.

members. The election came and went, followed by four years of political, social, economic, and medical turmoil—election 2020 aroused feelings of loss, anger, and fear. Old debates resurfaced just as new ones arose. Surprisingly, in the four years following the 2016 election, my brother went from a relatively apathetic political participant to an opinionated and involved one. If you have ever watched a nature documentary and seen two male bucks charging, rearing, and locking horns in battle, that is how my brother, Daniel, and I were with debates. Debates happened washing dishes, during outdoor fires, working out, and even via text.

These texts were like gas on a fire for me. They often came out of the blue and triggered rage within me. Topics ranged from DC statehood, fake news, and election fraud. Threads went back and forth with unverified claims, differing news articles that left my brother and I heated, angry, and dug into our beliefs; that is until my gratitude project. After practicing gratitude every day for a few months, I started to see a change in my approach to the debates. Daniel, for his part, was on his own faith journey that changed the way he approached arguments. Before, it was extremely difficult to listen and hear my brother's views. I started to appreciate his comments and the conversation. Don't get me wrong, I still got angry and disagreed, but debates left me less shaken and more invested in our relationships than before.

The first time I remembered transitioning from anger to gratitude was during a consistently debated topic as to whether the media was good or bad. In one instance, Daniel sent me a text with a link to an article and note, "Here is the problem with the media." Statements that the media was full of lies or ruining our country did not sit well for me. Freedom of speech, as in true news and journalism, are actually a core institution needed for democracy. My typical approach would have been to work through angry emotions internally and then respond with a relatively snappy text. However, in this instance, I started with gratitude.

To start with gratitude meant:

1. I thought about how grateful I was that we could have these debates and still love each other.

2. I was thankful for a country that allowed us to discuss our society and government without interference.

3. I was grateful my brother wanted to discuss these topics with me.

Feeling grateful three times laid a different foundation to the conversation than anger. Robert A. Emmons sees gratitude as affirmation and recognition. He writes, "It's an affirmation of goodness. We affirm that there are good things in the world, gifts and benefits we've received." And second, "We recognize that the sources of this goodness are outside of ourselves. We acknowledge that other people—or even higher powers, if you're of a spiritual mindset—gave us many gifts, big and small, to help us achieve the goodness in our lives."[28] Having practiced affirmation and recognition daily for over one hundred days by that time, made affirmation and recognition a reflex. Gratitude required that I affirm Daniel as a good person, not a political opponent. I recognized he gave me a gift by sharing his ideas, and I acknowledged

---

28 Robert Emmons, "Why Gratitude Is Good," Greater Good Magazine, November 16, 2010.

his views. The debate ended in gridlock, but it was not for nothing.

Gratitude did more than help me work through difficult debates. It strengthened our relationship. Gratitude researchers have found that gratitude positively influences relationships' quality and "can act as a booster shot" to maintaining healthy relationships.[29] Expressing gratitude on a routine basis is a way to maintain and foster healthy relationships. There is a "link between expressing gratitude to partner [friend, family, significant others] and feel increased communal strength in the relationship."[30]Daniel and I continue to have civil discourse on many topics. These disagreements only lead us to have more respect.

Life is full of harmful interactions and negative conflict. Through my days of gratitude, I still felt the full spectrum of emotions—anger included. However, gratitude made me resiliently flexible in my sentiments. It brought me back quickly to a state of homeostasis emotionally. Recovering rapidly from loss or conflict enabled me to turn to positive responses. This change helped me recover more quickly from bike theft or political differences. It helped me maintain and grow in relationships that had polarized viewpoints. Gratitude is a framework for reframing interaction into positive responses and outcomes.

---

29 Sara B. Algoe, "Find, remind, and bind: The functions of gratitude in everyday relationships,"*Social and Personality Psychology Compass*6, no. 6 (2012): 455–469.

30 Nathaniel M. Lambert, "Benefits of Expressing Gratitude,"*Psychological Science*21, no. 4 (2010): 574-580.

Living in Gratitude

Weeks before my gratitude journey, I felt like a broken rock: hard, jagged, and rough. My journey started as a way to "smooth" out my surfaces. Safely, I can say gratitude did change me. It has changed the way I interact with my closest relationships. Leading with gratitude caused a reciprocal environment of love and appreciation. Vocalizing thanks opened the door to public praise in teams, which created trust and collaboration. Adverse events were a venue to apply gratitude's reframing lens. Bad was still bad, but by acknowledging and finding pieces of gratitude, my reaction evolved. Conflict in relationships became less of an offensive onslaught and more a symbol of trust, love, and interest.

A few months after my project ended, my girlfriend and I were on a double date. In many ways, the project was a black box. I wrote, stamped, and sent "thank you" notes day after day. The notes' influence on the receivers and the world was impossible to discern. Knowing their impact was not the point of my project, but I'd be lying to say I was not curious if and how my notes changed the course of someone's day. Somewhere in between the sips of wine, my buddy's wife said, "Ever since Jamal (#8, #245, #343) received your 'thank you' notes, he has been writing more himself." "WOW!" is all that I could think. Hearing this was fantastic. To know that at least one of my notes encouraged someone to send their own meant that there might be others. Maybe my notes were like the skipping stone's impact on water, causing some ripples of appreciation.

Gratitude is an ongoing process (*a work in progress*, some might say). Like most things in life, my relationships with it have been in seasons. Some months, I was all in. Others it was just another task on my to-do list. However, the ongoing, consistent dedication to gratitude caused macro-level changes in my life. I cannot promise it will have these same effects for everyone, but there will be big picture adjustments. We have many people who come in and out of our lives. Leaning into the acknowledgment and recognition components of gratitude, we can appreciate each random relationship and realize its impact on us.

[**GRATITUDE OPPORTUNITY:** Write a "thank you" note to a person who has different viewpoints than you do.]

.03

a science

———

Mr. C,
Thank you for being a part of my life. I am blessed to have
met you at William & Mary. The way you attacked and
appreciated life always appealed to me. After you graduated,
I tried to carry on your spirit at school and in the club. You
continuously are serving others, which encourages me to do the
same in my own life. Thank you for your friendship.

MR. BROWER

Bro!
I just checked my mail and got your letter! You're awesome.
Fucking made my day.

MR. C

———

Blakely is my vibrant and loving five-year-old niece. My
love for her comes in part because she laughs at my jokes.
Recently, I taught her and her brother how to brain-suck
people. It was actually an accident. I like to palm my niece
and nephew's heads, move my hand like a jellyfish, and
yell, "Brain suck! Slurp, Slurp, Slurp." Making weird
sounds, wild hand gestures, and funny faces is an easy
way to catalyze voracious laughter with kids. Blakely
replicated the tricky brain suck maneuver on her mother.

I am proud to say I received the following text, "Did you teach my kids brain suck?" Yes, I can die a happy uncle. It is probably an overgeneralization, but by and large, kids approach life with simplicity. If it's funny, they laugh. If it hurts, they cry. The other day, I asked Blakely what she thought about gratitude.

Me: *"Why do you say thank you?"*

Blakely: *"Because it's good."*

Me: *"Why is it good?"*

Blakely: *"If we don't say thank you, then that is not nice."*

Her comment taught me that one, gratitude is deceptively simple. Two, she could write this book. Its simpleness is often mistaken for triviality. Despite, and partly *because* of gratitude's simplicity, it has a profound effect on our wellbeing. Gratitude is a straightforward concept, but its physical, social, and psychological benefits are not easily deduced.

In college, anytime I was assigned scientific articles to read, my eyes glazed over. If/then statements, math, and precise language were not my thing. Writing this book required me to seek quantitative, scientifically backed knowledge to support the concepts I noticed and felt. It turns out when I am interested in the topic, the science is rather compelling. Dr. Robert A. Emmons and Dr. Amit Kumar's work have deepened humanity's understanding of how gratitude impacts our wellbeing and why people have barriers to sharing gratitude.

Dr. Robert A. Emmons

Dr. Emmons published research, articles, presentations, and books over the last fifteen plus years. As the father of modern gratitude, he laid the foundation for research and experimentation. I learned the scientific side of gratitude by watching his Greater Good Science Center talks and reading *The Little Book of Gratitude*. His work boiled down gratitude's power to heal, energize, and change lives.

In Emmons' talk, "Gratitude Works! The Science and Practicing of Saying Thanks," he explains how it all started. Emmons was invited to a conference. The conference required that researchers became an expert on a topic. These new experts would then sit around a table and talk about the body of literature and their own findings. Emmons wanted to research humility because it was the inverse of what he was studying at the time, narcissism. A colleague, instead of him, was chosen to examine humility. By the time Emmons had a chance to choose a new research topic, gratitude was the only topic left. Serendipitously gratitude found him.

His objective for the conference was to know all the gratitude research and do some himself. He later said, "That was easy because it was about three studies."[31] Not wanting to show up to the conference referencing just three studies, Emmons rolled up his sleeves to learn more. Not getting his first choice at the conference became an excellent opportunity for him. The start of his relationships with gratitude exemplifies what he later concluded from his research. Gratitude helps us reframe potentially tricky situations.

One of his first experiments articulated the virtues of a consistent gratitude practice. Three hundred people

---

31 *The Table | Biola CCT*, "Gratitude Works!: The Science and Practice of Saying Thanks [Robert Emmons]," April 8, 2014, video, 1:11:59.

were randomly assigned to three groups. Group A wrote what they were grateful for in a journal daily. Group B wrote annoyances daily. Group C could write anything they wanted daily. Having done a gratitude journal of my own, I imagine they wrote things like morning coffee, a hug from a friend, and the beautiful sunset. If I had been in group B, I would have had an extensive list including people who ignored gym etiquette, played music too loudly in the subway, or chewed with their mouth open. Honestly, if I had been in group C, my journal would probably have been whatever was on my mind.

The findings were clear. Group A, the gratitude group, had a much higher well-being. They slept better and exercised more.[32] The study drove two main points. One, consistent gratitude is good. Two, structure is also good. Group A participants were given instruction to write any gratitude daily for a month. Structured but flexible activities lead to better results. This understanding helped inform my interest in developing a structured but flexible framework of my own.

What Emmons found in the journal study was just the tip of the iceberg. In his *Little Book of Gratitude*, he lists some of the "numerous psychological, physical, and social benefits [that] are associated with gratitude." These are important to document because it is easy to say gratitude benefits wellbeing, but more important to represent it with data.

- Keeping a gratitude diary for two weeks produced sustained reductions in perceived stress (28 percent) and depression (16 percent) in health-care practitioners.[33]

---

32 Ibid

33 Dr. Robert A. Emmons, "The Little Book of Gratitude: Create a Life of Happiness and Wellbeing by Giving Thanks (London: Gaia Books, 2016), 20.

- Gratitude is related to 23 percent lower levels of stress hormones (cortisol).34

- Dietary fat intake is reduced by as much as 25 percent when people keep a gratitude journal.35

- Writing a letter of gratitude reduced feelings of hopelessness in 88 percent of suicidal inpatients and increased levels of optimism in 94 percent of them.36

- Gratitude is related to a 10 percent improvement in sleep quality in patients with chronic pain (76 percent of whom had insomnia) and 19 percent lower depression levels.37

Gratitude, in some cases, is such an intangible concept, but Emmons brilliantly outlines a succinct and tangible definition. "Gratitude emerges from two stages of information processing—affirmation and recognition. We affirm the good and credit others with bringing it about."[38] Key learnings I draw from the explanation is that gratitude requires vulnerability. From the definition, we must look outside ourselves for a gift, which inherently means we did not deserve or acquire the gift ourselves. All accomplishments come to fruition with the help of others. However, rarely are people vulnerable enough to affirm others publicly who helped them succeed. Our society perceives vulnerability as a weakness; a symbol that we could not do it by ourselves. Gratitude

---

34 Ibid

35 Ibid

36 Ibid

37 Dr. Robert A. Emmons, "The Little Book of Gratitude: Create a Life of Happiness and Wellbeing by Giving Thanks (London: Gaia Books, 2016), 21.

38 Dr. Robert A. Emmons, "The Little Book of Gratitude: Create a Life of Happiness and Wellbeing by Giving Thanks (London: Gaia Books, 2016), 14.

inverses the narrative—celebrating the people who helped us on our journey.

Dr. Emmons dispels myths about gratitude. On first look, I wondered why this was necessary. After thirty-six interviews and having even more conversations for this book, I began to see that gratitude incorrectly applied to situations resulted in a negative connotation. For example, in one discussion with founders of a consulting firm that builds inclusive, equitable, and conflict adaptive workplaces, the idea of using gratitude as the foundation for difficult workplace discussion was vetoed quickly. They rejected it because gratitude may normalize existing power structures within an organization. People from specific backgrounds may be led to believe they should be thankful for just being in the room. In reality, their presence in the room should not be the main prize. The goal should be feeling comfortable to engage and invest in the discussion on *equal* footing. In my understanding of gratitude, I do not believe it could lead to the normalization of inequitable workplaces. However, the firm's founders make a very reasonable point that reverse phycology applied in the guise of gratitude can be a tool for oppression. The myth that gratitude leads to complacency is at the heart of the above example.

Naivety is another myth. I'm a glass-half-full type of person. When the pandemic hit, I continued to search for the silver linings. Spending more time with family, slowing down, and focusing on a small group of friends have been positive side effects of the pandemic. I was grateful for the renewed focus and simplification of life. That being said, I was still saddened by the hundreds of thousands of people who died from COVID. Was I naive in my gratitude? Some said I was. Others did not like when I asked them, "What are you grateful for in this difficult time of life?" These examples of complacency and naivety myths, in particular, highlighted to me the importance of sharing and debunking gratitude myths.

Emmons touched upon five myths in *The Little Book of Gratitude* that I feel are important to note. From my own 365-day gratitude journey, gratitude myths can be quickly dispelled.

1. **Gratitude leads to complacency.** My gratitude project ignited my curiosity, pushed me to research, engage with people, and write this book. No complacency there. One study shows that people who wrote down their goals and did a gratitude journal made 20 percent more progress on their goals than the control group.[39]

2. **Gratitude is just a naive form of positive thinking.** "Practicing gratitude manifests positive feelings more than it reduces negative ones."[40] Gratitude practitioners do not ignore negative feelings or events to find gratitude. Throughout my project, the pandemic started, systematic racism came into full view, and some politicians selfishly ripped apart democracy's most valuable institutions—speech, press, and elections. Even as positive emotions arose due to my project, I recognized the need to address many societal problems that arose in 2020.

39 Dr. Robert A. Emmons, "The Little Book of Gratitude: Create a Life of Happiness and Wellbeing by Giving Thanks (London: Gaia Books, 2016), 53.

40 Dr. Robert A. Emmons, "The Little Book of Gratitude: Create a Life of Happiness and Wellbeing by Giving Thanks (London: Gaia Books, 2016), 55.

3. **Gratitude makes us self-effacing.** Dr. Emmons discussed a study where participants were told they could win money by completing a difficult test. Then they were given a hint. Every participant recognized the hint was helpful. "Only those who felt personally responsible for their score felt grateful for the hint."[41] Being grateful for help others give does not preclude one from recognizing the value they themselves brought to an activity. Life is not a zero-sum game. We can be grateful for others' contributions while also recognizing our own.

4. **Gratitude isn't possible—or appropriate—in the midst of adversity or suffering.** I believe appreciation in difficult situations is a personal choice. A study by *The Journal of Positive Psychology* makes a strong case that gratitude amid adversity aids us in "feeling more closure and less unhappiness." Emmons studied this idea by working with individuals who had a neuromuscular disorder that left them in pain every moment of their lives. Subjects were asked to keep a gratitude journal. The ones that did had "significantly more positive emotions" than a group that didn't.[42] Gratitude is a valuable tool for every occasion.

5. **You have to be religious to be grateful.**[43] I believe this is a foregone conclusion. Even animals, who are probably not religious, "such as chimpanzees and

41 Dr. Robert A. Emmons, "The Little Book of Gratitude: Create a Life of Happiness and Wellbeing by Giving Thanks (London: Gaia Books, 2016), 57.

42 Dr. Robert A. Emmons, "The Little Book of Gratitude: Create a Life of Happiness and Wellbeing by Giving Thanks (London: Gaia Books, 2016), 60.

43 Dr. Robert A. Emmons, "The Little Book of Gratitude: Create a Life of Happiness and Wellbeing by Giving Thanks (London: Gaia Books, 2016), 63.

other non-human primates, seem to possess at least a more basic form of proto-gratitude, based on their ability to keep track of favors given to and received from different individuals."[44] Many religions promote gratitude through prayer and acts of service, but even atheists are allowed to be grateful.

The research clearly showed me that gratitude has a substantial impact in wellbeing. Fifteen years ago, gratitude was not on the radar of any major researchers. Dr. Emmons changed that. Now numerous studies and books express new learnings about gratitude. Yes, gratitude is a straightforward concept, as Blakely showed us. Though, in our world where data is king, having tangible quantitative and qualitative research on the subject allows us to have a deeper dialogue about gratitude's effect and possibilities. Emmons showed us that gratitude reduces stress, hopelessness, and pain while increasing happiness and health. Individuals and communities benefit from gratitude. Emmons' research gave me a scientific lens to view the positive improvements brought about by my gratitude journey.

Dr. Amit Kumar

There was and still is a stack of unsent "thank you" cards underneath my side table. Written years ago, they sit yearning to complete their gratitude mission. Over the years, after informational interviews, fun parties, or nice gifts, I wrote "thank you" notes with the intent of sending them. However, the intention shifted to apathy

44 Jason G. Goldman, "Gratitude: Uniquely Human or Shared with Animals?" *The Thoughtful Animal* (blog), *Scientific American*, December 1, 2010.

when I couldn't find an address or stamp. While missing addresses and stamps were the usual villains, occasionally fear prompted me to stall. On one occasion in summer 2014, I interviewed for a job. After the interview, I excitedly wrote a note, filled the envelope, addressed it, and stamped it. Before sending it, I decided not to send it. The fear that the note would be too much or seen as brown-nosing stopped me.

The insecurity related to my estimation of the note's reception was not isolated to me. Amit Kumar (#171) and Nicholas Epley published *Undervaluing Gratitude: Expressers Misunderstand the Consequences of Showing Appreciation.* The research explores the question of, if people know gratitude is good, why are there not more letters sent?[45] Curious about this question, I contacted Amit for an interview in summer 2020.

During our interview, I found a very gentlemanly soul, dark brown hair, and a voice that rose with curiosity when exploring his own and his partner's research about pro-social behaviors. He elaborated on how they came to research gratitude: "It seems intuitive people get it [gratitude], this message [gratitude is good] has been put out there for a while, and yet people aren't doing it all that often. That made it just curious as to why." Amit went on to hypothesize that when people think about gratitude, "They might think they're doing something small when actually it's much more meaningful for the recipients." I continued to think about my unsent notes as he talked about his research. What Kumar and Epley found was really interesting.

---

45 Amit Kumar and Nicholas Epley, "Undervaluing Gratitude: Expressers Misunderstand the Consequences of Showing Appreciation,"*Psychology Science*29, no. 9 (June 27, 2018): 1423-1435.

Expectations and competence are two potential reasons why there is a relatively low amount of gratitude, per our knowledge of its values.[46] Lowenstein Camerer and Martin Weber find that givers often believe their recipient already knows about the gratitude, making expressing it unnecessary.[47] Or, as Kumar and Epley stated, "[This perception] would lead expressers to underestimate surprise in a gratitude recipient."[48] They found that givers tend to judge interpersonal acts based on competence, whereas the receivers assess them based on worth.[49] Our world is full of luxury and material things. It is sometimes hard to realize that small acts, such as gratitude letters, have substantial worth. These learnings gave me a new perspective on the relationships between the giver and receiver. Their findings are based on a group of 107 MBAs.

Kumar and Epley asked students to email a gratitude letter to someone. Students then made a few predictions. The letter recipients were surveyed with slightly altered questions after reading the letter.

- How surprised the recipient would feel getting the letter (zero being not at all surprised to ten being extremely surprised).

46 Ibid

47 George Loewenstein et al., "The Curse of Knowledge,"*Journal of Political Economy*97 (1989): 1232–1254.

48 Susan T. Fiske et al, "Universal Dimensions of Social Cognition,"*Trends in Cognitive Sciences,*11 (2007): 77–83.

49 Amit Kumar and Nicholas Epley, "Undervaluing Gratitude: Expressers Misunderstand the Consequences of Showing Appreciation,"*Psychology Science*29, no. 9 (June 27, 2018): 1423-1435.

- How the letter would make the recipient feel (negative five being much more negative than normal to five being much more positive than normal).

- If the recipient would feel awkward reading the letter. (zero being not at all awkward to ten being extremely awkward).

Senders were vastly incorrect. On average, the MBAs underestimated their recipients' surprise and positive mood upon reading the letter by one to two points. Students overestimated how awkward a reader would feel by two points. The gratitude receivers did not feel awkward and were more grateful than expected.[50] Kumar and Epley continued experimenting, running four with various tweaks. The learning gained from the experiments paint a fascinating asymmetric relationship between givers' predictions and receivers' responses. I latched onto three main points that resonated with me based on my experience:

1. A giver's estimations of the recipient's emotions are strongly related to the desire to express gratitude.

2. Givers overestimated the importance of a skillful expression of gratitude, which can become a speed bump for giving appreciation. In reality, the receiver is much more concerned with the intention, not competency.

3. "Expressers also significantly undervalued the positive impact of their gratitude on recipients."[51]

---

50 Ibid
51 Ibid

Sometimes in my project, I thought a recipient would feel awkward receiving gratitude. I pushed passed this psychological barrier by imagining, if nothing else, my note would make the recipient smile. Consistently the recipient was not awkward. They were actually excited. The encounters led me to believe there were similarities in my "thank you" notes and Kumar's letters. Kumar reminded me, "We had people write letters of gratitude. Those are potentially more meaningful, potentially more important than a simple, 'thank you' note." Even though Kumar and Epley didn't study "thank you" notes, my antidotes line up with his research. Take for example, a note to an ex-girlfriend.

A few years back, I dated a woman who lived many states away. It didn't work out. And no, not because I tried the brain-suck thing. When I began my gratitude project, I thought she'd be an excellent person to thank. But Facebook quickly confirmed she was recently married. Cue my apprehension. Would she actually appreciate the note? Still, in the end, I sent her a quick Facebook message. "Hey, it's been a while, but I'm doing a gratitude project...I promise it's not anything weird. Would you be comfortable sharing your mailing address with me?" She confirmed my account was not hacked and then gave her address. Upon receiving my note, she sent a short but sweet "thank you" message back. Without my gratitude project, I would not have sent the note because I would have assumed she wouldn't appreciate it. Her response was a great example that gratitude is valued more than we would expect.

Kumar's research shows that giving gratitude consistently ends better than the sender believes. Even though

I have had my fears sending gratitude, consistent positive feedback has trained me to work through the fear. When in doubt, send gratitude. Kumar said to me, "I think the powerful realization is that the simple kind of seemingly small changes in how we approach life can make a big difference when it comes to how we feel and how we treat others." Gratitude affords us the opportunity to actively live better and be better. Our conversation ended with him saying, "I like to think of what I study as an attempt to get a better understanding of our everyday lives and how those lives can be improved." Kumar's work empowered me to recognize gratitude's impact is more than we predict. Next time when considering leaving a "thank you" note unwritten or unsent, think (thank) again.

Gratitude is Good

Looking back at the origin of my gratitude journey, loneliness was a main catalyst. I had no clue how potent gratitude could be for one's wellbeing. My mind just craved it. Somehow my body knew I needed it to improve my psychological, sociological and physical health. Even though gratitude can be sliced and diced by research, it is innately human. Science will never take the place of actively participating in gratitude—just ask Brian Doyle, John Kralik, A.J. Jacobs, Hailey Bartholomew, and my dad. I saw the various research components throughout my project and can attest to their validity. Truth be told, I wanted to avoid writing about the science of gratitude because it sometimes makes gratitude feel less personal. That being said, the research is profoundly interesting and provides substantial evidence of gratitude's positive outcomes. In fifteen years, I hope Blakely can look back at this chapter and realize she had it all right—gratitude is good—and there is research to back it up.

[**GRATITUDE OPPORTUNITY:** Write a "thank you" note to someone who you see every day, but don't often notice.]

PART 2

.04

a mindset

———

Joneses,

Thank you for raising such an incredible son. I have been blessed to have Cameron in my life since freshman year. He is a man of his word, loyal as a friend and a hard worker. Throughout the years, we have stayed in touch. I continue to learn from him. I know we have only met a few times, but your parenting has developed a person whose friendship I hold close.

A. BROWER

Big dog Austen,
Thanks for the thoughtful note that you sent to my 'rents. I'm not sure what you put in it, but they really and truly appreciated it. Thanks for being such an epic, consistent friend over the years—you da man!

CAMERON

During summer 2020, I was an MBA intern at American Express. I interviewed for the position at HQ in New York City. My interview room sat at an elevated sixty stories above Manhattan, providing vistas of the Statue of Liberty and the Empire State Building. Real conversations took place, meaning my interviewers did not just drill me with questions. Instead, they explored my background, their experiences, and opportunities with the company. I sent each interviewer a "thank you" note that expressed how pleasant the interview was and how warm it made me feel. A few months later, as an intern, I spoke with Julia, one of my interviewers. Julia told me at the candidate review meeting, she displayed my note to aid the discussion on my application. By no means did the note alone get me the job, but it had become part of my story.

"Thank you" notes have always been part of my career story. As a young professional, I was surprised to find most "thank yous" sent to interviewers were not reciprocated. I had no clue what happened to the notes in many cases, nor did I hear from the companies. Did the notes make it to the interviewers? The least these companies could do was tell me I didn't get the job. Looking back, I realize that 1) sending a "thank you" note with ulterior motives was wrong, and 2) it was inappropriate for me to have sent expectations along with the notes.

As a gratitude practitioner, it was vital to have few expectations and a firm grasp of "why" a project was done. Setting one's mindset helped. My year of gratitude solidified the importance of setting a mindset and four other learnings. These learnings became my five-step framework to build a gratitude ecosystem.

1. **Set the Mindset**

2. Tie to Talents

3. Identify Stakeholders

4. Prepare & Simplify Deployment

5. Reflect & Celebrate

Phase 1 of building a gratitude ecosystem is to "Set the Mindset." I believe this is the most important phase of the framework because it informs the other ones. As in any endeavor, maintaining a constructive mindset establishes a successful tone. Framing the mindset ensures the right mentality for a consistent gratitude practice. To set a mindset requires 1) reflecting on the "why" behind a gratitude project and 2) addressing project expectations.

Why am I Doing a Gratitude Project?

Simon Sinek's 2009 TEDx Talk, "Start With Why," became the third most-watched on TED.com, inspiring millions of viewers to think differently. The video now has over fifty-three million views. In it, Mr. Sinek drew a bull's eye with three rings. Next, he scrawled "why" in the center ring, then "how" in the middle, and "what" in the outermost. Sinek goes on to say that people and leaders typically start with "what." He says if Apple were like everyone else, they would say, "[What] We make great computers. [How] They are beautifully designed, simple to use, and user-friendly. Want to buy one?" But, based on their trillion-dollar market cap, they are not like everyone else. Instead of starting with "how," they start with "why." "[Why] Everything we do, we believe in challenging the status quo. We believe in thinking differently. [How] The way we challenge the status quo is by making our products beautifully designed, simple to use, and user-friendly. [What] We just happen to make great computers. Want to buy one?"[52] Starting with "Why" allows

52 *TEDxPugetSound.* "Start with Why -- How Great Leaders Inspire Action | Simon Sinek | TEDxPugetSound," September 29, 2009, video, 18:01.

companies and people to have the right focal point for "how" and "what."

My "why" was not created in a day. For months, I had been feeling emotionally raw and without direction. Waking up feeling horrible after a night out pushed me to the edge but gave me the nudge I needed. Unable to do homework, I had the mental space to piece together reasons behind my negative emotion and potential solution. All this to say, "whys" take time to develop and careful consideration. The work put into creating the "why" will pay dividends throughout the gratitude project. So, concerning a gratitude project, what is the "why" behind it? Is the purpose to change perspectives? Is it to revitalize old and start new relationships? Is the "why" the pursuit of happiness? No matter how or what the gratitude project is, finding the "why" is the most crucial part. "Why" bleeds out into the "how" and "what." As Simon Sinek would say, "Start with 'why.'"[53]

The "why" that drove me began with the idea that living life pursuing the fading delights of partying had me focused on things I did not value. Every note, within my gratitude project, was an activity to reframe my life so that my actions were in the service of others. Until watching Simon Sinek's video, I could not put my "why" into words.

- [Why] In everything I do, I believe I can push myself to be more self-aware and have an eye toward celebrating others.

- [How] The way I push myself is by making consistent time to reflect, consider peoples' positive impacts, and celebrate them.

---

53 Ibid

- [What] I just happen to share gratitude with "thank you" notes.

My "why" drove me. Some days I woke up without gratitude in my heart. When I felt that way, I reminded myself that the project was a stretch goal and something bigger than myself. At the end of the semester, MBAs are simultaneously involved in organizations, recruiting for jobs, and taking exams. A heavy schedule left little room for even dinner. In spring 2020, that was my workload. It was easy to wake up and go to school without stopping to write a "thank you." Setting my "why" at the beginning helped inspire me to write notes even in a busy time.

Sinek's framework can be applied as a lens to view other gratitude projects. Thinking back to the projects described in Chapter 2, each practitioner's "why" was unique. Kralik heard a voice in the mountains. Bartholomew pursued happiness. A.J. answered his son's challenge. These "whys" enabled the practitioner to deliver consistent, genuine gratitude. The "whats" and "hows" are interesting but don't dictate each project's success. "What" they were doing was all the same—sharing gratitude. "How" they did it varied. Kralik and my dad wrote "thank you" notes. Bartholomew took pictures, and A.J. emailed, called, and met people.Thinking back to my gratitude journal, I never clearly defined my "why." I believe that is why the project failed. It's important to note I like Sinek's "Start With Why" theory. However, the concept may not work for everyone. No matter the framework, having a "why" to start a project is the key.

Brian Doyle's "why" is one of the most potent examples of a clear "why" leading to a successful project. During our conversation, he reflected, "The purpose [of the project] was as somber as it sounds. If I died the next day, there would be no questions as to how I felt." The depth of his "why" transferred into his "how." When sharing gratitude, he pushed deep within himself as to why he appreciated someone. "It's hard to be specific. I think people are very used to just saying 'thank you' so much. 'You're amazing.' 'You're my best friend.' 'Thank you.' And I would try to challenge myself each time. What's the 'why'? Why are they amazing? Why are they my best friend?" Doyle completed his first project in 2013 and launched the second year of gratitude in August 2020. I was lucky enough to be his forty-seventh "thank you," the second time around. His intention, depth of gratitude, and authentic compliments left me speechless and must have filled up his cup too.

My dad's "why" was based on relationships. "It's all about building a brand for yourself and who you want to be, how you want to follow up, your consistency, your detail, and your level of interest." Each person's "why" is a highly personal decision that has downstream effects on the gratitude project. As one considers becoming a gratitude practitioner, spend time exploring the reasons. Setting the mindset starts with the why.

Manage Expectations . Enjoy the Journey.

My brother is five years older than me. He was always taller, stronger, smarter, and better at games than me. The claw game is one of the games that I could not beat, and he could. Walking into smokey old pizza places, bowling alleys, or even movie theaters, the irresistible opportunity to win toys, video games, or candy always caught our eyes. Game after game, we would watch him position the claw with precision, moving it ever so slightly. His entourage, myself, my sister, and friends grew queasy as the game clock ticked down. With a press of the red button, the claw plunged into the treasures! The anticipation was usually more overwhelming than the result. Usually, the claw came up empty. On occasion, it pulled out the prize only to drop it halfway up. With my brother in the driver's seat, our persistence sometimes paid off with toys. We would return home like kings and queens with prizes held high!

A few days would pass, the prizes lost their shine and landed at the bottom of the toy chest. To this day, I could not tell you what toys we earned, but I can recount the happiness of being together and enjoying the process of getting the prize. It's not a perfect analogy, but the claw game is very similar to how I felt about writing "thank you" notes. It was always fun to get a prize, (in this case, a "thank you" note,) but the real joys were distributing "thank you" notes and having the conversations they triggered. Looking back, it truly was the process that I enjoyed, not the responses. Whenever I expected some-one to respond, and none came, it left me feeling disap-pointed and less excited about the project.The twelfth "thank you" I sent helped me learn management of expec-tation was valuable.

Agora, a Mediterranean restaurant in Washington, DC, was Christina's and my favorite. Walking in, one is trans-ported to another world by the dimly lit room, soft red glow, conversations, and laughter. Plates appear in front of guests by an inconspicuous army of servers. Tender morsels of food fall apart in one's mouth. On a date in February, we had the best waitress ever, Vessela (#12). She was kind, funny, and decisive. Christina and I wrote a note that expressed how welcomed we felt and how she made our night special. Having been a server myself, I know they do not receive much praise outside of notes on receipts and tips. Because of this, I expected to get a response or some free drinks the next time we ate at Agora. No answer came, nor did we receive free drinks at our next meal. Upon realization that I would not get anything in return, my mood soured.

When the recipient did not meet my expectations, I became less excited about the gratitude project. The bizarre negative emotions prompted self-introspection. My twelfth note did not embody my "why"—to celebrate others. It started from a good place but turned into entitlement. Reflection helped me see my mistake. I had inappropriately and disingenuously sent gratitude with expectations. Attaching expectations to my note left me open to becoming disappointed in my recipient. That was unfair. If I genuinely wanted to celebrate others, I needed to ensure I sent no expectations with the notes. Learning this early on, I repositioned my mindset. No longer did I have expectations for the recipients or specific project outcomes.

Much of the gratitude project was sending and not receiving. After the Agora incident, I grew to find beauty in that. Grade school teachers got notes that elaborated on how their class changed my life with no response. Transactional situations with bus drivers, waitresses, and hotel staff prompted me to give notes. Many family members, friends, ex-girlfriends, and ex-co-workers received cards with no response. These individuals did not return my note for one reason or another, including, for some, the belief that a "thank you" card marks the end of an interaction. Without expectations, the joy of reflecting and giving gratitude was the focal point of my actions. No longer could expectations interfere with my "why" or the positivity I wanted to share with others. Managing expectations helped me enjoy the whole journey.

During my year of gratitude, roughly 80 percent of people did not respond, and 20 percent of people sent a text, made a comment, or returned my note kindly. Returned notes, calls, or texts brightened my day and added gas to my gratitude tank, but they were just added bonuses. Many media sources discuss how gratitude projects result in economic success, better relationships, stronger friendships, and numerous other benefits.[54] These outcomes are wonderful. But if one expects every gratitude expression to come back, generating reconciliation and powerful experiences, they are going to be severely disappointed. Gratitude, at its core, is a monotonous pursuit for consistent appreciation of others, which is valuable in itself. It is essential to recognize that somebody may not be ready for gratitude, or maybe they're not going to be thankful until five to ten years down the road. Setting one's mind to have realistic expectations will help manage a gratitude project's emotional ups and downs.

Phase 1: Set the Mindset

I firmly believe that Phase 1: Set the Mindset is the most crucial part of building a gratitude ecosystem. To do

---

54 Amy Morin, "7 Scientifically Proven Benefits Of Gratitude That Will Motivate You To Give Thanks Year-Round," *Forbes*, November 23, 2014.

something well, one must first understand why one is doing it. Second, managing expectations ensures focus on the "why" and not unrealistic outcomes.When starting a gratitude project, take the time to home in on the "why" and develop clear expectations. Like in the claw game, I grew to anticipate just playing with gratitude. My main tool for gratitude was sending it via "thank you" cards, but that didn't stop me from texting it, saying it, writing it, or even hugging to show gratitude. No matter the response to my different types of appreciation, I enjoyed the process. In the book *The Way of The Peaceful Warrior*, Dan Millman reminds us, "The journey is what brings us happiness not the destination." A mindset composed of a compelling "why" and little expectations helped me enjoy the journey.

[**GRATITUDE OPPORTUNITY:** Write a "thank you" note to yourself. What do you appreciate about your body or mind?]

.05

a recognition

———

Hello Smiths,

It has been a while since the Tough Mudder and the incredible Italian dinner you all made for us. I had a blast getting to know you both. As well, thank you for raising a wonderful and kind son. It was a pleasure to get to know him at William & Mary and as his senior year roommate. Your son is a dedicated, loyal, and humorous friend. He certainly helped make my senior year at school and continues to as a supportive friend.

Best,

A. BROWER

Hi Austen!

It's Annmarie Smith. We received your lovely note. What a thoughtful gesture! I happen to be missing my boy, so your timing was perfect and put a huge smile on our faces! Hope all is going well with you and that we see you soon. Please thank your parents from us for raising such a wonderful and thoughtful human being! Wishing only the best things in life for you, Austen!

Best,

ANNMARIE & JULIO

———

For as long as I can remember, wherever I went, I liked to make new acquaintances. At my college dining hall, we had the same ladies, Melody and Jen, swiping our student access cards. After a few visits, I was on a first-name basis, knew their kids, and a few fun facts. We would joke around, making every dining experience that much more enjoyable. Developing relationships with people like Melody and Jen who were often overlooked was fulfilling. So many students treated the women swiping our cards as machines, barely making eye contact. Noticing everyone and making an attempt to let people know they were seen was something I valued. After witnessing many of my interactions, one of my best friends said to me, "The crazy thing is you actually care about meeting them." To have someone reflect that I was genuine in my brief relationships meant a lot.

The gratitude project constantly evolved. The one constant was ensuring all people, even those often overlooked, could be part of it. Giving gratitude should not be kept selfishly to close connections. Therefore, I imagined everyone—baristas, friends, ex-girlfriends, and waitresses—as stakeholders in the project. Expanding my perception of those involved allowed me to lean into my relationship-building talents and kept the project intriguing. When I think about the five phases of the framework, phases 1–3 have to do with strategizing and 4–5 the act of doing. Phase 1 is the "why" behind the project. Choosing how one will give gratitude happens in Phase 2. Phase 3 recognizes who is involved. Once the "why" of the project is set, the "who" and "how" can follow.

1. Set the Mindset

2. **Tie to Talents**

3. **Identify Stakeholders**

4. Prepare & Simplify Deployment

5. Reflect & Celebrate

Phase 2: Tie to Talents

Clifton StrengthsFinders changed the paradigm in how individuals and workplaces understood themselves. StrengthsFinders is a personality assessment that celebrates people's strengths (talents) and directs them to strengthen talents versus focusing on weaknesses. "It isn't until people know what makes them talented and unique that they know how to perform better...."[55] Don Clifton, the founder of StrengthsFinders, clarifies talents as "Naturally recurring patterns of thought, feeling, or behavior." StrengthFinders tells us, "To turn those talents into strengths, you must *invest* in them—practice using them and add *knowledge* and *skills* to them."[56] Investing in and using talents is also an extremely effective way to stay energized and happy within gratitude projects. Hearing other gratitude practitioners' stories and reflecting on my own, I had the realization that the best projects were intertwined indirectly or directly with peoples' innate abilities.

There are only a few activities in my life that I felt excessive joy and flow doing. I think I am a talented wrestler. When wrestling, I had a purpose and felt that I was born to do it. Knowing I am good at something made me want to do it even more. It may be surprising to learn (or it might not be) that I never considered myself talented at

55 Gallup, "CliftonStrengths Explains How You Are Uniquely Powerful," accessed January 15, 2021.

56 Gallup, "Talent X Investment = Strength," accessed January 15, 2021.

writing. Even while writing this book, the intricacies of grammar and tenses made me feel like a fourth grader attempting to avoid the teacher's eyes during grammar lessons. All this to say, even though I wrote "thank yous," my talent was not in writing. As defined by Clifton StrengthsFinders, my strengths or talents are responsibility, includer, positivity, futurist, and connector. Three out of five—includer, connector, and positivity—are relationship-building skills. I believed my talent was to connect, develop, and maintain relationships persistently. "Thank you" notes were just the vehicle to do so.

My talents were loosely associated with the specific act of writing. I viewed "thank yous" as opportunities to maintain relationships and start new ones. "Thank you" notes allowed me to use my strengths. As an includer, I used the four-ripple framework (discussed below) to make sure I wrote "thank yous" to everyone. As a connector, I enjoyed writing "thank yous" to new relationships and secondary relationships. As a positive person, writing positive affirmations to other people was in my wheelhouse. "Thank yous" were the vehicle by which to leverage my strengths. Thinking back to my gratitude journal, it was just writing. Just writing did not employ my strengths and therefore failed. If a project does not support one's skills, it may not be successful.

As opposed to my indirect use of talents, Hailey Bartholomew and Jo Englesson are excellent examples of directly using talents. As a professional photographer, Bartholomew was talented at taking pictures. Each day she used her talent to capture something she was grateful for with a photograph. I have never met Hailey, but I imagine connecting photography with her gratitude project made it feel more familiar and enjoyable. The results speak for themselves. She completed 365 days of gratitude in 2009 and inspired thousands through her story, Instagram, webpage, and book.[57]

Jo Englesson, the founder of TOFA (Token of Appreciation), published *Source Movement*, a book on gratitude, and is the proud owner of Gratitude.com. She told me about her journey, which started by almost bowling over an elderly gentleman in a Florida airport. The man, Don Warms, responded to the collision with kindness. Sitting with the feeling of gratitude, Jo decided to act. She leveraged her years in software engineering to build a website that could track physical tokens of appreciation. Thus, TOFA's were born to be "handed to someone that makes a difference in your day and then tracked on the Token Travel Map." Jo gave her first token to Mr. Warms in 2007 and continued giving one every day for a year. Englesson's talent was software engineering. She made a website to track, manage, and spread her project. Tying her gratitude project to her talent led to incredible results. There are more than thirty thousand tokens in circulation today. That is a lot of appreciation.[58]

Investing in and using talents for a gratitude project is an effective way to stay energized, engaged, and happy. Consider using talents directly or indirectly in a project. A direct use is when the act of gratitude is the talent. For example, a baker could bake a cake for someone they appreciation once a month. An artist could paint

57 *Tedx Talks*,"365 Grateful Project | Hailey Bartholomew | TEDxQUT,» September 2014, video, 12:04.

58 Jo Englesson Bio, "Bio | Jo Englesson," Jo Englesson, accessed February 23, 2021.

portraits of people they appreciate every few months. A barista could make a free cup of coffee every week with a kind message written on the cup. An indirect use is when the act of gratitude just connects with a talent. For example, a soft skill like maintaining relationships connects with writing "thank you" notes. A skilled thinker can send voice messages over the phone.

Gratitude is more than a "thank you." It is an action and mindset with profound effects when applied with the right tools. By tying gratitude to talents, the gratitude shared will be more genuine and effective. Importantly, I believe tying a project to personal talent will lead to more enthusiasm and likelihood of success.Phases1–3 set up a gratitude project's "Why," "How," and "What." Basically, a practitioner sets their project mindset and then designs the project based on their talents. Deciding which community of potential recipients to focus on is the practitioner's next step.

Phase 3: Identify Stakeholders

By June 2020, I had sent over 150 notes. Each morning became an exercise of reaching deep within my memory to find a new recipient. Without a playbook to rediscover people in my past, I felt like I was continually recycling and writing to the same people. Around this time, I found out that the human brain can only remember roughly 150 names and faces. "There is a cognitive limit to the number of individuals with whom any one person can maintain stable relationships," Robin Dunbar Emeritus, Professor of Evolutionary Psychology at Oxford, infers in his research.[59] Amusingly, I had arrived at my ceiling of easily accessible names. It would take a plan to break through my brain's natural limits.

One weekend that summer, I sat on a deck overlooking mountains drenched in green foliage with a fresh coffee. Friends still slumbered inside the cabin. My mind, body, and spirit were in a contemplative mood. Till that day, I had not attempted to categorize my notes into thematic areas. Each note was a very personal and specific recognition to someone. "How could I generalize such personalized interactions?" I thought. Maybe it was the view, the coffee, or the fun weekend with friends, but I was able to step back and look holistically at the types of people who received notes. Four categories or ripples revealed themselves:

- Ripple 1: Friends, family, and mentors

- Ripple 2: Members of my life's story

- Ripple 3: Daily interactions

- Ripple 4: Secondary relationships

When thinking about the four categories, my mental picture was of a stone plunged into calm waters. I was the stone. Each category rippled from me. The ripple closest to the center contained people I wrote to first, such as family, friends, and mentors. The next ripple was filled with individuals from my life history—old teammates, ex-girlfriends, classmates, and other acquaintances. The third ripple was one of my favorites. These were people I came in contact with every day or serendipitously.

---

59 Mona Chalabi, "How Many People Can You Remember?"*FiveThirtyEight*, September 23, 2015.

Bus drivers, front desk people, or restaurant servers are there. The outermost ripple held secondary relationships. People who drastically affected my life, but in a secondary fashion. Think LinkedIn second connections. The ripple contained people like my best friend's parents and my parents' best friends. These categories became the foundation for my recipient discovery process.

When considering who to write a "thank you" note to, I would think through each ripple. When my project first started, the easiest people to write to were family and friends. So, I started there. As days rolled by, I sent notes to people further from the center. The four-ripple playbook worked. No longer was I waiting for a name to pop up in my mind. Using the four ripples as a prompt helped me look outside the 150 names my brain could handle. Choosing recipients in the morning became easier. The categories or ripples provided personas by which to guide my thoughts. Here are a few examples to help prompted exploration.

Friends, Family, and Mentors

Matt (#29) is one of my best friends. We met at the College of William & Mary. As freshman hallmates and senior year roommates, we had our fair share of memories, including Matt making up raps about friends or late-night milkshake runs. Matt returned home to New Jersey after graduation, and I settled in Washington, DC. Time created distance, but not separation. My note to him was simply a recognition of friendship and his importance to me as a person. He responded a few weeks later with a customized "thank you" note that had his initials across the card's cover. Matt started with, "Thanks for the card, homie. It made my day to read your kind words. I often find myself thinking back to our boggin' days." He signed off, "You were a great example of how to be bold and connect with people." I shared this not to tout what a bold, connected person I am but to exemplify how gratitude often comes back when put into the world.

Family, friends, and mentors are some of the easiest names to come up with and respond with the most personal notes from my experience. Because I had the most frequent interactions with this group, many received two to three notes through the year. Sending multiple notes per person helped grease the wheels of my gratitude project. No one seemed to have issues with receiving more than one note.

Members of my life's story

Nathan (#131) and I met in high school. We only hung out during the wrestling season. Wrestling Nathan was like wrestling a blacksmith. His hands were more like hammers, and a one to two-minute match left me with a pounding head. I respected him as a wrestler and person. We had not spoken for eleven years, but he came to my mind one day, so I sent him a note. A week or two later, he responded. A wolf's grin and squinting eyes commanded the cover of his note. Nathan wrote, "I am truly honored you took the time to send me a card. I write back to you to show my appreciation and the value of your friendship." He went on to invite me to Montana.

Nathan's response solidified for me how you treat others will not be forgotten. We had respected each other in high school, and that respect and kindness carried through eleven years to a genuine card and invite. Writing to people in this category was fun because it took me down memory lane. Some of the responses were the most surprising because we often picked up the conversation where we left off. Time is not an issue when sharing gratitude.

Daily interactions

The bus to my university follows a constant loop between two stops. It starts at Dupont Circle and ends at Georgetown University. Each bus driver toils on the same pavement day after day. One bus driver (#5), in particular, turns the fifteen-minute drive into a joyous opera and jovial pump-up speech. As you enter the bus, in a booming, baritone voice, he welcomes you. "Welcome, great to see you today" or "Hello, beautiful person!" During my year of gratitude, I carried notes with me everywhere just in case. That particular late January morning, I had yet to write my note. A few blocks from the destination, I scribbled the note as best I could between the moving bus's jig and jag, then licked the envelope. Departing the bus, I handed him the note, smiled, and walked off. The note contained my appreciation for the care and excitement he brought to my morning.

Mr. Bus Driver never mentioned the "thank you." In particular, the serendipitous nature of this ripple meant there was often no contact with the recipient after handing off the note. I felt these notes were particularly fun because of the randomness and likelihood that I would never see or hear about how the note impacted them.

Secondary relationships

Mr. Davidson (#51) grew up with my father. They attended college in Oxford, Ohio, on the brick-laid streets of Miami's campus. As lifelong friends, I have, time and time again, witnessed their relationship bond. Now, as a young man, the strength of their friendship and its impact on me came into clarity. My "thank you" note outlined how Mr. Davidson's involvement in my dad's life shaped how I interact with my friends. To close, I said how much he meant to my dad. Davidson never said anything to me, but he mentioned it to my dad. A long conversation or journey through their shared history did not follow, but they savored the gratitude together. My dad described the situation. "You know, I really think it was kind of a savoring moment for him. I think that the acknowledgment and appreciation was so meaningful that they just left it at that."

I call these secondary "thank yous." Writing indirect thanks to someone influential in a close connection's life is very different than writing direct gratitude. Secondary notes require the writer to empathize with their primary connection while keeping in mind the secondary relationship. This triangular thinking makes these notes unique out of the four-ripple playbook. Responses to these notes were often emphatic coming from the primary and secondary connection.

These four categories represent people who are stakeholders in my life journey, albeit to varying degrees. I found giving thanks to everyone, from a bus driver to my best friend, maintained my focus on gratitude throughout the day. Anyone could be a gratitude target. Emmons' definition of gratitude consists of recognizing and acknowledging people for the gifts they give. My gratitude project underscored that all people gave me gifts, even if it was just a smile or conversation. Life would not be possible, fun, or engaging without everyone in it. Gratitude helps us recognize that. For me, using these ripples helped to simplify the recipient decision-making process. As a reminder, there is no one correct way to do it. These ripples are just an initial playbook for someone starting a journey.

What's Next?

Considering direct and indirect talents for my project was a good opportunity for self-reflection and an enjoyable way to deploy my abilities. Thinking about applying skills to a concept in Phase 2 was challenging. I would typically think about leveraging talents in athletics, the arts, and a professional setting. Within Phase 3 it was fascinating to categorize people within my community. By tying the project to talents and identifying stakeholders, a practitioner will be ready to distribute and celebrate gratitude!

Phases 4–5 simplify the deployment process and create space for reflection and celebration of the experience.

[**GRATITUDE OPPORTUNITY:** Write a secondary "thank you" to a parent's friends.]

.06

an expression

———

Hello Mr. & Mrs. Farehills,

It's been a pleasure to get to know you both over the years. Thank you for always opening your home to me. I'll never forget the weekend we all came up from Williamsburg to hang out. You and Joe made incredible flank steak for dinner with all the fixings. I am blessed to have become friends with your son. He has made a difference in my life and many others. The apple doesn't fall far from the tree.

Best,

A. BROWER

Hi Austen!

Thank you so much for your heartfelt note. It made our day. Truly. These past several weeks, I've found myself reflecting on many things, including the special people that have become part of our family over the years. You're certainly one of those people. We love you and hope to be able to see you sometime. Please know that if there's anything you need, we're here and happy to help, whether it's answering health questions or concerns (Joe's department), cooking, baking, books, or math (my department), or—well—just anything else. Keep in touch.

Much love,

THE FAREHILLS

Late spring 2020, amid the pandemic, Christina and I moved from San Diego to her parent's house in Prescott, Arizona. By this time, I had read John Kralik's book, so my content had improved. The cards themselves were simple but classic. Anyone seeing them would know I had been intentional about my choices. It was in Arizona that I started to think, "How can I make these notes more special for the receiver?" I thought about what I could add to the envelope. Wax seals always seemed distinguished to me. I remembered when my friend, Andrew, a lover of history and wax seal enthusiast, sent me a letter with a wax seal. It was regal, thoughtful, and differentiated the letter in my mind. What says to someone, "You are important to me," better than a wax seal?

One quick trip to Jo-Ann Fabrics later, I had the tools needed to wax seal my notes. Wax seals helped me to celebrate my recipient by showing them they warranted the extra step. The added weight and texture brought uniqueness. I loved the significance seals added, but they came with difficulties. By choosing to use wax seals, I raised the time and resource barriers needed to distribute my notes. No longer could I write, address, stamp, and then send a note. Wax, heat, and time were required. Thus, my distribution slowed. I needed to figure out a way to prepare and simplify deployment to stay on track.

Phase 4 includes preparing and simplifying deployment. Phase 5 creates space for reflection and celebration of gratitude experiences. Together they conclude the framework ensuring gratitude is given and enjoyed.

1. Set the Mindset
2. Tie to Talents

3. Identify Stakeholders
4. **Prepare & Simplify Deployment**
5. **Reflect & Celebrate**

Phase 4: Prepare & Simplify Deployment.

Junior year of high school, my teacher, Mr. Hapner (#13), brought US History alive. He would take measured steps in front of the class and hold his pointer finger and thumb to his chin thoughtfully as stories poured from his mouth—Hapner's control of historical knowledge and ability to tell stories held us at attention. I credit Mr. Hapner for my love of American history, especially the Civil War. Abraham Lincoln conducted the management of the war. A master communicator and tactician, Lincoln used notes for various reasons, including preparing and deploying orders. Lincoln did all within his power to prepare the country and army for war. He knew that preparation was key to victory. He once said, "Give me six hours to chop down a tree, and I will spend the first four sharpening the axe."[60]

A gratitude project is no different than cutting down a tree. Preparation is vital to simplify the deployment of gratitude. I learned the hard way the importance of preparation. Early in my project, I made the mistake of only purchasing ten or twenty-five cards at a time. As one might imagine, cards flew out the door (daily). Maintaining a stash of cards was especially challenging when I was apt with my dyslexia to switch a few letters on the card or envelop; thus, killing that card's opportunity to be sent. When writing to an old boss who had been

60 "Abraham Lincoln Quotes," BrainyQuotes, accessed February 21, 2021.

important to my professional development, I burned three cards due to fatal errors, including incorrectly writing my address and misspelling keywords. Running out of "thank you" notes would halt my gratitude project for a couple of days until purchasing more.

In my project's early months, I consistently ran out of notes, stamps, and wax seals. From my experience, any obstacle to sending gratitude, no matter how small, became overwhelming when thinking about it over a year. It's not the first time that small obstacles blocked productivity. Research shows that workplace obstacles, even excess approvals and meetings, inhibit employees and create strife.[61] Awareness of the study and feeling how these small barriers affected me, helped me pre-empt them. I started to buy large quantities of supplies and had a standing order on Prime to avoid slowing my momentum. Being prepared with the right supplies kept me on track to completing 365 days of gratitude.

When I think of this phase, I think of Hailey Bartholomew, Brian Doyle, and John Kralik. On the preparation front, Bartholomew knew she wanted to take 365 photos throughout the year. She prepared by purchasing 365 days' worth of film. Thus, she would never lack the tools necessary to deploy her gratitude. Concerning deployment, Doyle was adamant about completing gratitude every day. He said to me, "For some reason, I forced myself to do it [sharing and blogging] each day before midnight. I would not allow myself to do it the next day." I was not able to be as disciplined. Learning that famous practitioners, like John Kralik, were comfortable

---

61 Lucas Pols, "Leadership: The Importance Of Removing Barriers Facing Your Employees," *Forbes*, January 2, 2019.

missing a day and making it up later gave me relief. Having leeway on what "daily" sometimes meant gave me the flexibility I needed to enjoy the project. It never became a burden.

Preparation simplifies deployment and creates an environment where quick, consistent deployment of gratitude is easy. It increases the probability of a completed project. Preparation put me in a position where all I needed was someone's address to send the note. Removing barriers such as low supplies maintained momentum. Whether the practitioner chooses to send a "thank you" note, talk to everyone in the supply chain, take photos, or blog, specific materials, including time, are needed to sustain the campaign. So, when planning a project, remain prepared. Sharpen the axe.

Phase 5: Reflect & Celebrate.

During the first months of the gratitude project, I was heads down in school and completing my daily gratitude ritual. The notes' content was okay but lacking. Sometimes I sent more of a token versus a thoughtful expression of my gratitude. Not until I started writing this book and reading John Kralik's did I take the time to reflect on my gratitude expressions. I soon realized my notes missed depth. Kralik's "thank you" notes were rich with examples and emotions. In his book, he shared a few. "Thank you for being cheerful and happy when I pick you up in the evening. Sometimes I don't have a very fun day, but when I see you, and we talk about things and have fun, I feel better. Thank you for being the best daughter ever." Another read, "Knowing that you had to work on Thanksgiving, of all days, I thought I'd express my gratitude that you have taken the time and made the effort to learn my name and greet me each day in a way that makes me feel like a person instead of a number. It's a small thing, but on any given day, it can make all the difference. Thank you!"[62]

Reading Kralik's book provided the perspectives I needed to see gratitude expressions differently. His book encouraged me to reflect at a micro and macro level. On the micro-level, I considered the quality of my previous notes and made the choice to improve future ones.before Kralik's book, a note to a mentor would have been pretty simple: "It was a pleasure to work with you and learn from you this summer. I hope to see you again in the fall." After I incorporated reflection into my process, my notes became animated. For example, "Over the summer I was blessed to meet great people at American Express. I am most thankful for being introduced to you. Thank you for speaking to me on multiple occasions, providing advice, and teaching me about storytelling. Your advice to estab-lish key mentors and really get into the details of what people do directed me throughout the summer" (#182).

On the macro-level, I thought about my whole journey. What was it doing to me? How was it impacting others? What I began to realize was that gratitude is a work in progress for all the participants. A beta reader (#44, #224) for this book mailed me a note. She said that after reading my book, she had written more "thank yous" than ever before. Various interactions like this underscored

62 John Kralik,*365 Thank Yous: The Year a Simple Act of Daily Gratitude Changed My Life*, read by John Kralik, London: Penguin eBooks, 2011, Audible audio ed., 5h 18m.

the web of gratitude created by the project. However, the realization would not have come without reflection during the many stages of the gratitude project. Therefore, I made it a point to add reflection into Phase 5 of my framework.

Reflection helped me identify opportunities for celebration. I celebrated my journey by telling its stories. For example, Christina and I went out for a date night. We ended up at the DC restaurant Gypsy Kitchen. Having a nice night, our spirits were high, and the jokes were rolling. The waiter, Grant (#231), relished our energy. He responded to jokes, told stories, and probably hung out with us too long compared to his other guests. The interaction was one of the best dining experiences I have had. Grant and I exchanged numbers.

He received a "thank you" note and was appreciative via text. Grant texted, "I got your letter today, and I just wanted to say thank you. Like seriously, thank you. I can't express how much seeing that today brightened up my day. You didn't have to do that, and the kindness that you and your girlfriend have extended to me is honestly more than I expected but it's exactly what was needed if that makes sense. With that all said, again, thank you, and I hope that you both come back to GK soon because having a friendly face and good banter would be great on a regular occurrence." I love telling the story because it is fun and somewhat unexpected. Grant would want people to find joy in our conversation. By talking about it, I am able to celebrate him and gratitude, while also igniting inspiration in others.

Celebration prompts me to recognize that gratitude brought new memories or deepened relationships. A friend of mine, Frankie (#119, #129, #160), and I spoke about "thank you" notes during a bike ride. I celebrated gratitude by telling him a story of a note I had written to an old manager. Making conversation, I asked if he ever received a "thank you" note. Frankie said no. Since then, Frankie and I have swapped notes three times. By sharing gratitude through stories, he now writes "thank you" notes. I hope he finally receives one from a mentee. To be clear, I don't go up to people and say, "Hi, my name is Austen, and I have written 365 'thank yous.'" But if gratitude comes up and I have a relevant story, I share it.

Reflection is key to foster productive improvements in a gratitude project. Reflecting improved my notes and expanded my perspectives on my project. Celebrating is important fuel. Telling and celebrating gratitude stories is another way of spreading gratitude. Even just hearing someone else's "thank you" can trigger a chain reaction of appreciation. Reflection and celebration are Phase 5 of the framework but should be active throughout. By reflecting and celebrating, one is more likely to continue working on gratitude, but as always, *Gratitude: Is a Work In Progress.*

A Five-Phase Gratitude Framework

Each note I sent became part of a tapestry of gratitude. That tapestry helped me realize the framework seen below. I can't take credit for the framework without acknowledging the individuals who shared their addresses, sent a response, or called. Phase 4 and 5 are the action-oriented phases of the framework. They are the phases that bring smiles, build connections, and turn people into epicenters of pro-social behavior.

1. Set the Mindset

2. Tie to Talents

3. Identify Stakeholders

4. Prepare & Simplify Deployment

5. Reflect & Celebrate

I had an unusual feeling when I designed the framework. A year of gratitude boiled down to five simple steps. There was something beautiful in the simplicity. Though, there were elements that could not be captured; components of the journey that can only be experienced, not shared through storytelling. My five phases of gratitude for building a gratitude ecosystem are just a blueprint, meant to be iterated upon; each step flexible enough for creativity while also structured enough to be a guide. I hope whoever uses the framework will think about the 365 notes and various stories it took to create it.

[**GRATITUDE OPPORTUNITY:** Write a "thank you" to your parents.]

PART 3

.07

an opportunity

———

Mrs. W,

It's been a while. You may not remember me, but I look back fondly on you and your class. For some reason, I have a detailed memory of writing "I wish I were a _____" poems and using the microscopes in the back of your class. Thank you for making my fifth-grade experience really great. I am blessed to have had you. Your teaching has made me a better student and person.

Best,

A. BROWER

Austen,

It is wonderful to hear from you! Of course, I remember you and your sister too. You have a wonderful family, and I enjoyed being your teacher. I remember your mom and dad too, as I remember visiting your sister when she was ill...How is your family, and are you in college or working? We are in school and have been since August. We are working hard to stay healthy, and we all wear masks all day. I'm starting my thirty-first year of teaching. How old are you? I will go to school tomorrow and look up your picture in my old yearbook.

Thank you so much for the nice note.

MRS. W

———

Mrs. W (#107) was my fifth-grade teacher who taught me how to write poetry. My favorite poem at that time, probably because she liked mine, was an "I wish" poem.

These poems started with "I wish I were X." The rest of the poem articulated why that was the case. The first poem I wrote was "I wish I were an ocean big blue and free." During the poetry week, the middle school had an assembly to show gratitude for school volunteers. Our class wrote poems for the volunteers. Strategically, I wrote my next poem, "I wish I were a volunteer." Somehow, I was chosen to present during the assembly. The assembly taught fourth and fifth graders that they should appreciate all individuals, including volunteers, that make the school a better place.

When my gratitude framework was effective in a personal setting, I started to wonder whether it could be applied elsewhere. As I pondered other arenas, I thought about Mrs. W's poem segment. It reminded me that I learned gratitude, recognition, and acknowledgment in school. As an MBA, I started considering how the framework could be applied within a business and a classroom. As one will see, plenty of research indicates gratitude improves efficiency, retention, and well-being in both contexts. Having not tested my project in either, I used research and interviews to examine the idea. Using people and institutions that already exercise gratitude, I will apply my framework on top to give an example of how it could look.

Five-Phase Framework In Education

First, I am not a teacher, but I have been in school for over nineteen years, seen many educators, and have been a part of innumerable classrooms. Educators have a tough task to manage students in the school, administrator, and state standards outside of it. I believe gratitude projects can be integrated into existing curricula and classroom rituals to improve student engagement, build community, and improve learning outcomes. The following example provides context to how the framework could look. I spoke with an educator, a first-grade teacher, Mrs. Bree, about how she would use my gratitude framework. Her gratitude project would have students write "thank you" notes to someone every Monday during community circle meetings. Let's take a look.

Phase 1: Set the Mindset

Mrs. Bree has a holistic mindset when it comes to education and community. She values teaching the whole person and working to bring all stakeholders together. Mrs. Bree explained to me that expectation setting, from an educator's perspective, is usually related to classroom norms such as respect and not talking while others are talking. She recommended I clarify how I use expectations. In the gratitude framework, expectations are used to represent the anticipated outcomes of the project. Mrs. Bree's "why" and expectations for the project would be clear.

- [Why] I am an educator to improve the whole person and community, not just teach subjects.

- Expectations: Engage the entire educator community, including students, teachers, administrators, and parents, using gratitude.

Phase 2: Identify Stakeholders

Defining the stakeholders in the educational setting would be very important to Mrs. Bree. To fulfill her "why," leveraging everyone in the educational ecosystem would be crucial. Here are the stakeholders she identified.

- Ripple 1: Friends, family, and teachers
- Ripple 2: Members of her students' educational story
  - Peers, educators, administrators
- Ripple 3: Daily interactions
  - Cleaning staff, volunteers, mailman, presenters, bus drivers
- Ripple 4: Secondary relationships
  - Friends of parents, the teachers' parents, etc.

Phase 3: Tie to Talents (curricula or classroom rituals)

Educators are talented at developing a holistic curriculum and structured classroom environment. Educators could tie the gratitude project to students' talents, existing curricula such as grammar lessons and "thank yous," or classroom rituals like daily community circle. In Mrs. Bree's case, she would connect gratitude to Monday Community Circle Meetings. Kids sit cross-legged while they receive an update for the day and participate in group activities. For the gratitude project, her students would join the community circle on Mondays, learn about a different stakeholder each time, and then write a "thank you" note to that stakeholder. By connecting the gratitude project to existing rituals, students will more easily adopt the project.

Phase 4: Prepare & Simplify Deployment

When we talked about Phase 4, her voice rose. Her speech quickened with excitement. She laid out a plan for preparing a gratitude project that fully engaged the various stakeholders.

1. The teacher (herself): Prepare a lesson on a different stakeholder before every Monday. Have a clearly defined plan about how much time to give the project each week and how long to make it. Develop and print gratitude sentence stems for the students to complete their "thank you" note. Something like "I am thankful that you _____. The school would not be the same without you."

2. Parents: Provide an overview of the project to parents. Express to them that the project will require their support. It could be to complete "thank you" note delivery or coordinate mailing.

3. Students: Communicate with students that they are expected to bring pencils and draft paper each Monday. Involvement and attention would be required during the Monday meetings.

4. Administrators, other staff, (including bus drivers and cleaning staff): Notify them about the project and ask them to consider responding in kind to the students if they receive a "thank you." Invite some of them into class for brief presentations.

By preparing the materials and stakeholders, the project would be simple to deploy and likely result in students receiving more responses.

Phase 5: Reflect & Celebrate

Mrs. Bree was excited about the idea of doing the gratitude project for the whole month of November. Ending the project on Thanksgiving would provide ample opportunity to celebrate the project during the annual Thanksgiving party. Students could tell a story about their favorite "thank you" note experience while listening and reflecting on their peers' stories.

Mrs. Bree mentioned that each teacher approaches classrooms and students differently. If a "thank you" note project is not an educator's style, here are a few other projects to consider. Greater Good Science Center outlines activities to blend appreciation into the classroom, including gratitude journals, gratitude visits, daily or weekly "thank you" notes, three minutes of gratitude, or gratitude circles.[63]

- A gratitude journal is a daily practice of writing down three to five gratitudes on a regular cadence.64

- Gratitude visits are when students write a letter of gratitude to someone in their life, then read it to that individual, and return to class sharing their experience.65

- Three minutes of gratitude is reflecting on gratitude at the end of the day for three minutes. A group of students gathers weekly in a "circle" to share what they are grateful for.[66]

63 Susan Fountain et al., "Nurturing Gratitude From the Inside Out: 30 Activities for Grades K-8," Greater Good Science Center (2017): 4.

64 Ibid

65 Ibid

66 Ibid

Gratitude projects like the one Mrs. Bree described have many benefits. "When students are thankful, they feel more connected to their schools and teachers," say researchers Jeffrey J. Froh and Giacomo Bono.[67]The duo was one of the first to research gratitude in schools and developed the first Gratitude Curricula.[68]

Their studies "found that teens who had high levels of gratitude when entering high school had fewer negative emotions and depression and more positive emotions, life satisfaction, and happiness four years later when they were finishing high school."[69] Another study found that "feeling grateful motivates adolescents to help others and use their strengths to contribute to society."[70]Further, gratitude's impact is not temporary but lasting. In a longitudinal study, Bono's team found gratitude increased subjective wellbeing, decreased depression, increased hope, and greater meaning in life four years later.[71]Teachers already leave lasting impacts on their students. By adopting gratitude in the classroom, a teacher's life-changing impact may be more than an education, but an increase in wellbeing and purpose for years to come.

To be completely honest, at times the gratitude projects were difficult to do myself. Attempting to teach gratitude to a classroom of students sounds daunting. Perhaps, though, that is why I am not an educator. My hope is

67 Jeffrey Froh et al., "How to Foster Gratitude in Schools."*Greater Good Magazine*, November 9, 2012.

68 Gratitude Curricula, "Gratitude Curricula | Greater Good Science Center," Greater Good Science Center, updated October 11, 2020.

69 Jeffrey Froh et al., "How to Foster Gratitude in Schools."*Greater Good Magazine*, November 9, 2012

70 Ibid

71 *Greater Good Science Center,*"How Can We Cultivate Gratitude in Schools?" September 29, 2014, video, 17:19.

that the steps above can serve as a flexible guide. Educators know their students, parents, and schools better than anyone. They will be able to evolve the framework accordingly to leave lasting impact on their students.

Five-Phase Framework In Business

"The Mighty is a digital health community created to empower and connect people facing health challenges and disabilities." Mike Porath, the CEO, started The Mighty after learning his "Two-year-old daughter had a rare chromosome disorder, Dup15q syndrome." In the first year of the business, The Mighty reached thirty million people. Appreciation and gratitude helped Mike's team grow the external community and foster a great internal one. Their lucky break came when early on, a story went viral reaching six million people around the world. The story had a link at the bottom to "Submit your own story. Become a Mighty Contributor." With so many eyes on the article, they began to test iterations. "One thing we tried got five times the amount of traffic leading to submissions for us...Write a 'thank you' letter to someone who has helped you on your health journey. Submit it here." Story submissions went from ten to fifteen a day to hundreds.[72]

Appreciation helped to grow the external community. Gratitude helped to keep it. The Mighty started long before I created the five-phase framework, but if we were to apply the five-phase framework to their existing gratitude infrastructure, how might it look? The Mighty team

---

72 *CMX*,"3 Million Registered Users. Zero Marketing Dollars | Mike Porath," October 7, 2019, video, 22:04.

already sends "thank you" notes weekly.Let's explore the project with the five phases lens.

Phase 1: Set the Mindset

Having a daughter with a rare chromosome disorder left Mr. Porath grasping for research or techniques to work with her. He found one PDF article written by another parent from a similar situation.[73] Having someone else, outside of doctors, who understood the situation and could provide guidance, meant the world. Mike created The Mighty to make sure kindred spirits, going through difficult health experiences, could find one another. As we now know, gratitude is a phenomenal lubricant for community. If Mike were to have set the gratitude mindset for his company's "why," it might look something like this:

- [Why] Acknowledge, recognize, encourage, and connect people facing health challenges and disabilities.

- Expectations: A supportive community that shows gratitude and appreciation for others.

Phase 2: Identify Stakeholders

The Mighty was created to consider anyone who was thrown a curveball.[74] The four-ripple framework could be used to define the stakeholders. Here is an example of how The Mighty team might use the framework to consider all stakeholders.

- Ripple 1: The Mighty team members

73 Ibid

74 "Who We Are | The Mighty," The Mighty, accessed January 21, 2021.

- Ripple 2: Members of The Mighty community
  - Suppliers, vendors, writers, and community members
- Ripple 3: Daily interactions
  - Cleaning staff, mail people, public transit staff
- Ripple 4: Secondary relationships
  - The Mighty team members' partners, mentors, friends

Phase 3: Tie to Talents

At the core, The Mighty "started as a publisher, but is now more a network," Mike said to me during our call. Writers, editors, and digital technology people make up the majority of the organization. So, it is not a stretch to assume the company has core competencies (or talent) in writing. Tying a gratitude initiative to writing would be a good idea since the employees are already good at it. Therefore, the gratitude project chosen was for the employees to write weekly "thank you" notes to stakeholders.

Phase 4: Prepare & Simplify Deployment

Gratitude does not directly keep the lights on. That being said, The Mighty integrated gratitude creatively to prepare and simplify its deployment. A community standards team supports millions of members. Since that team has the best sense of the community, they were the ones aggregating names to be sent "thank yous" and set up the weekly "thank you" note sessions. Each week the group sat down and wrote gratitude. Therefore, within the framework, the community standards team would focus on Phase 4 to prepare materials and send the notes for the whole Mighty team.

Phase 5: Reflect & Celebrate

Since "thank you" notes would be written together and done consistently, the weekly meetings would be a great time to reflect and celebrate gratitude. Team members could talk about who they were writing a "thank you" to and why. They could tell stories and share the response they received during the week. The simple act of writing, reflecting, and celebrating would enhance their community of over three million users, encourage positivity within the community, and increase employee happiness.

The Mighty team already does employ gratitude consistently. On any given Friday, The Mighty employees write "thank you" notes to their community. Over twenty thousand have been sent. Now the organization has over two million registered users. I would argue the external community was built, in part, on gratitude.[75]Mike and I spoke a few weeks before the holidays. He was in the process of writing a "thank you" note to every employee, thanking them for their work over the year. Mike and his team write notes to each other and consistently consider gratitude. It has become part of workplace culture. Employees love The Mighty, putting their heart, soul, and skill into their work. Other companies may want to consider making gratitude a more significant part of workplace culture based on the average workplace retention and culture numbers.

---

75 *CMX,*"3 Million Registered Users. Zero Marketing Dollars | Mike Porath," October 7, 2019, video, 22:04.

In 2019, when unemployment was at an all-time high, a study found that less than 50 percent of people felt they were in a good job.[76] Dissatisfied employees lead to turnover. Turnover is expensive. "The cost of losing an employee can range from tens of thousands of dollars to 1.5–2.0x."[77] Overwhelmingly, the struggling leaders I have met and worked with are not trying to sabotage their company's culture or employee retention. More often, they want a positive work environment and satisfied employees. The 2018 Global Talent Trends study by Mercer identified three components that correspond to great places to work: permanent flexibility, commitment to health and wellbeing, and working for a purpose.[78]

Components two and three, commitment to health & wellbeing and working for a purpose, can be improved by applying gratitude. Developing a company's gratitude ecosystem will help reinforce a commitment to health and well-being and bolster employees' purpose. I have two caveats. If an organization has problems, just being more grateful will not clear up the situation. Gratitude can help leaders see, hear, and appreciate employees at work. Two, organizational culture change is challenging. It will not change overnight. If the majority of the organization doesn't get on board, things won't change. The power of gratitude is a great place to start for organizational change because it is relatively simple. People are already are doing good work.

76 Jack Kelly, "More Than Half Of U.S. Workers Are Unhappy In Their Jobs: Here's Why And What Needs To Be Done Now,"*Forbes*, October 25, 2019.

77 Jack Altman, "How Much Does Employee Turnover Really Cost?"*HuffPost*, January, 18 2017.

78 Alan Kohll, "What Employees Really Want At Work,"*Forbes*, July 10, 2019.

Through my gratitude project, I have seen gratitude increase wellbeing, deepen relationships, and improve communications. Gratitude certainly influenced The Mighty's culture and community. Company norms are deeply embedded within organizations. To alter them requires intention and thought. I think it is important to note that the adoption of gratitude can be implemented within organizational value systems or by individual managers. Either way, consider adopting gratitude in the workplace.The framework has not yet been tested in a corporate context. However, based on my research, interviews with gratitude consultants, and experience, applying my five phases will change a culture.

Gratitude Thrives In Many Places

Greg Kenney served as the President and CEO of General Cable from 2001 to 2015.[79] General Cable's HQ is in Northern Kentucky. A billion-dollar company with interests all over the world, Greg worked seven days a week taking calls from the US, Europe, Africa, and Asia. I spent the day with Greg in 2010. He was the first CEO that I had ever knowingly met and definitely the first one to invite me into his office. At the time, I didn't understand the responsibility on Greg's shoulders. To me, he was just my uncle. To be honest, as a senior in high school, the last thing I wanted to learn about was the cable industry. (I almost fell asleep reading General Cable briefs in his office—don't tell.) But looking back, I learned something fundamental—appreciate everyone.

---

79 "Gregory Kenny - Member of Board of Directors @ AK Steel," Crunchbase, accessed October 10, 2020.

Throughout the day, Greg and I had a chance to talk and see different parts of the company. In the kitchen, he spoke knowingly to the staff. A kind "Hello!" was given to everyone he passed in the halls. He treated his secretary as family. When he wanted me to understand the business's customer service side, he asked a manager on the team, by name, to let me shadow him. Greg, the CEO of the multi-national and multi-billion-dollar company, noticed everyone from the cleaning staff to the senior leaders. Greg noticed and recognized everyone.

My gratitude framework can be used to aid in the development of a more grateful culture in the board room or classroom. Imagine if everyone, from top to bottom, of a business or school, noticed all the stakeholders that made it function. That would be the place I want to work at or go to school.

[**GRATITUDE OPPORTUNITY:** Write a "thank you" note to a teacher from your K-12 experience *and* write a "thank you" note to the cleaning staff at your office giving your appreciation for the clean environment they make.]

.08

a work in progress

_____

Mom,
Many stories and conversations that we had about gratitude
were in the chapters that I cut to shrink my book's scope. I did
not want to write my first book without featuring you in some
way. You have been my biggest advocate and strongest writing
influence. When my college essays were not good enough, you
edited them. When I needed more people to beta read this
book, you did. Thank you for always being there, supporting
me, helping me grow, and guiding me. I see your influence in
so many of my actions and could not be more appreciative
that your influence is always with me.

Love,

YOUR SON.

365 days passed quickly. The world changed a lot between January 26, 2020, and January 26, 2021. A new president was elected, I got a dog, and I started a job at an incredible startup company—Poppy Flowers. The only element that didn't change was the weather. A year later, Washington, DC, was still grey. Leading up to the project's end, I never thought about it. The notes had no expectations, which left me without any anticipated outcomes. After I addressed my 365 notes, I set my pen down. Internally,

I smirked. Around the apartment, no confetti fell, and social media was silent. No lightning bolt of enlightenment struck. The world didn't seem to notice. All this felt right. The shifts, successes, and celebrations happened slowly throughout the journey.

Some of the most significant shifts in my thinking occurred after unexpected discussions that left me wondering whether my project was honorable. Conversations on the virtue of gratitude left me feeling exposed. Had my pursuit of sending positivity and building community been self-serving acts? One interviewee's last words were, "I wouldn't want to receive a 'thank you' note from you if you are going to write about it." I am now very much at peace but feel these discussions are unavoidable. More so, they are essential to have because they drive conviction and promote action. Even as I celebrate the end of this book and call people to gratitude projects, I feel it's vital to question whether gratitude is a virtue.

Virtue or Vice

As my dual journeys of writing this book and finishing a year of gratitude unfolded, I had many conversations about gratitude with friends. One text sat unread in my inbox for eleven days. The text was a request for information. "Nonurgent question. What is the value of gratitude? Not flippant. Trying to articulate it more clearly. An alternative phrasing of the question—what is the virtue of gratitude?" I let the question steep. The sender, Jobe, was a friend of philosophical thoughts. Gratitude's moral nature was on trial! My pending response became better articulated in person. Is gratitude a virtue? This question and subsequent conversations would shake my confidence in the gratitude project's core.

Sitting in my living room having beers, Jobe (#117, #294) and I struggled with gratitude. He wondered how gratitude could be a virtue if the act of giving gratitude was not entirely altruistic. "You as the sender get a ton of benefits from sending a 'thank you' note." This was the first real pushback on my project. I had blindly believed my notes were, at the worst, acknowledged then thrown away. Never had I dreamed of them as selfish acts. I responded to Jobe, "Virtuous acts do not have to be fully altruistic. Sending 'thank you' notes make me feel good, and others feel good. The notes were never sent with solicitation, which would indicate a clear selfish intent." We carried on till midnight with no clear conclusion. However, later in the week, I was told by someone else since I was now writing a book about my gratitude project, it disqualified the gratitude notes; implicitly saying my "thank you" notes were tainted because I would tell their stories in a book.

Plenty of holistic acts that result in personal gain are still considered virtuous. If a doctor saves a life, were they not being virtuous because they were paid? If someone networks a friend into a job interview, were they not virtuous because they received the halo effect of supplying a good candidate? If a person chooses to love someone, is love not virtuous because they selfishly gain comfort and support? In my view, all these slightly selfish acts of altruism, friendship, and love, are virtuous. Because gratitude is an innately human activity with resounding positive effects, there is no way around receiving kickbacks (big or small) from giving gratitude. Setting the appropriate selfless mindset (Phase 1 of the gratitude framework), non-virtuous and selfish acts of gratitude are avoided. I believe gratitude is virtuous. Does that mean it's altruistic?

The real question is: Can altruism, "The belief in or practice selfless concern for others' well-being," be slightly selfish?[80] Janice Kaplan, in her book *The Gratitude Diaries: How A Year Looking On the Bright Side Can Transform Your Life,* shared with her readers a year of living in gratitude. Kaplan mentioned a story about her friend trying to build a relationship with her daughter. When her friend started texting her daughter gratitude versus advice, their relationship improved. Selfishly, her friend wanted to connect with her daughter. Altruistically, she wanted her daughter to succeed in life. In the story, Kaplan hits upon gratitude's duality. "Gratitude doesn't need an immediate reply. You did it [sent gratitude] for yourself as much as for her."[81] The altruistic act of giving gratitude is acknowledging another. It's okay to feel good about it. So, in response to my friend, Jobe, and the gratitude crisis, I do care that my "thank you" notes may be perceived as selfish. However, my intention and expectations are the only part of the equation I can control. With the right intent, the sender and receiver of gratitude gain.

Jobe's points facilitate great discussions. There are many good conversations around gratitude's virtues and society's expectations of it. My feeling is that if done genuinely, people feel good. That is enough for me. When many hear about giving gratitude every day or the inclusion of

---

80 *Oxford Languages Online*, s.v. "altruism*(n)*," accessed January 21, 2021.

81 Janice Kaplan,*The Gratitude Diaries: How a Year Looking on the Bright Side Can Transform You Life*, read by Janice Kaplan, London: Penguin Publishing Group, 2015, Audible audio ed., 8h 12m.

gratitude practices within daily rituals, they often think, "What's the catch? What are you getting out of it?" I felt it critical to my credibility as a gratitude practitioner to address those concerns. Some people take advantage of gratitude. Just read Adam Grant's book *Give and Take* to learn more about takers.[82] Just because givers of gratitude benefit does not mean giving gratitude is inherently wrong. Ultimately, it is up to the readers to decide if the benefits of making other humans feel good, recognized, and acknowledged outweighs the potentially iniquitous nature of gratitude. For me, it does—and I have 365 reasons to back it up.

Curious and Brave

January 2020 started as a normal year but turned into a rough one. COVID put humanity into a box. For me, that was a first-floor apartment in Washington, DC. Days rolled by on my computer with little human interaction. With my gratitude project in full swing, every socially distanced interaction was a conceivable "thank you" note. That mindset gave me a much-needed community in a lonely time. The front desk people (#128, #155) and mailman (#57) received "thank yous" and became friends. I started to notice garbage pickup was Monday, Wednesday, and Friday around 7:30 a.m. Each morning, the garbage man (#242) and I waved through the window. He received a "thank you" note for noticing me. The garbage man and his driver now wave and honk every time they stop by. The pandemic forced life online where connections and communications were instant. Even so,

82 Adam Grant, "Give and Take: A Revolutionary Approach to Success," read by Adam Grant, London: Penguin Audio, 2019. Audible audio ed., 6h 56m.

gratitude placed me in a position to develop an unexpected community when I needed it most.

The journey and positive results were serendipitous. Gratitude became a tool to deal with the stress and vitriol of the shaken world. Three hundred and sixty-five "thank yous" paved the way for honest dialogue between politically opposed family members. It revived relationships with old friends. I formed new relationships with strangers, such as the waiter at Gypsy Kitchen (#231) and professors (#319). Gratitude's positive influence in a very lonely and distanced world helped to sustain my project. "Since lockdowns and stay-at-home orders were instated, roughly a third of American adults report feeling lonelier than usual, according to an April survey by social-advice company SocialPro."[83] Sharing positivity and deciphering gratitude in a world of hurt prompted this book and its big "Aha!" A simple, consistent gratitude mindset leads one to action, to remember what others do for them, and to capture everyday moments to give appreciation.

Science has shown us that these everyday moments of appreciation increase the well-being of individuals and community. For example, "Keeping a gratitude diary for two weeks produced sustained reductions in perceived stress (92 percent) and depression (16 percent) in health-care practitioners. Writing a letter of gratitude reduced feelings of hopelessness in 88 percent of suicidal inpatients and increased levels of optimism in 94 percent of them."[84] Whether a child or adult, gratitude evokes awareness of humanity's unique reliance on

---

83 Jamie Duchame, "COVID-19 Is Making America's Loneliness Epidemic Even Worse,"*Time*, May 8, 2020.

84 Dr. Robert A. Emmons, "The Little Book of Gratitude: Create a Life of Happiness and Wellbeing by Giving Thanks (London: Gaia Books, 2016), 20.

others. Gratitude is the kindling for humanity's resilient spirit. Simply put, there is no better time than now to exercise one of humankind's most innate responses to external behaviors.

Gratitude is good, but that does not always make it easy. Applying the concept for a year, better yet, a lifetime, is a daunting idea. I failed many times throughout the project, just as I have failed many times as a person. I sent "thank you" notes with expectations. Sometimes weeks went by without sending a note. In a few instances, people did not want my gratitude and felt it inauthentic. I learned that striving to prevail was the exciting part of gratitude and life. Even though gratitude is a simple concept, applying it frequently, in a structured manner, can be intimidating. Gratitude practitioners, including myself, followed a structured practice to give gratitude consistently. I made those learnings into a framework. The five-phase framework was designed to facilitate success.

1. **Set the Mindset** - Declare a "why" and manage expectations.

2. **Tie to Talents** - Design a project based on personal skills.

3. **Identify Stakeholders** - Determine possible recipients of gratitude.

4. **Prepare & Simplify Deployment** - Clear potential barriers to success.

5. **Reflect & Celebrate** - Contemplate and share the experience.

These simple steps can be adapted to fit one's lifestyle and gratitude goals. The framework will help identify a gratitude project's goals and objectives, establish an

A WORK IN PROGRESS · 127

advantageous medium of delivery, and liberate gratitude from one's heart. The five-phase framework for developing gratitude ecosystems can be deployed personally or within various communities.Surprisingly, I didn't start writing the book knowing the framework. Reflection on my gratitude journey and the incredible stories of others aided in the development of it. The five phases can be adapted to meet anyone's needs.

Living in an MBA and business world, frameworks for decision making, organizing, and analyzing were pervasive. Sometimes to elicit organization or community change, a structure clarifies the process. The five phases of a gratitude ecosystem can be adopted by professional organizations like a business or nonprofit. Educational environments such as a classroom or school may also employ the framework to boost community, productivity, and wellbeing. What's surprising is that even if the organization doesn't formally adopt the framework, an individual practitioner within the community can use gratitude to inspire a halo of appreciation within the institution.

Some naysayers may push back on gratitude, feeling it is a fluffy concept. As a person, who relishes the power to act and the result of those actions, gratitude is not fluffy. Hearing how daily gratitude texts saved a mother and son's connection, how Hailey Bartholomew revitalized her romantic relationship with her husband, and how John Kralik turned around his life and business, gratitude is anything but fluffy. Conversations and unique perspectives often elicited new feelings and emotions about the project. Naysayers contend that writing a book decreased my gratitude notes' value and that gratitude is a selfish act. Allowing my emotional response and the science to guide my perception of gratitude, I confidently say gratitude, given genuinely, has benefits for the receiver and the giver. Gratitude is an act of acknowledgment, recognition, humility, and creation that changes internal dialogues and perceptions.

Creating anything, a website, art, business, or relationship, requires creative destruction, followed by rebuilding. My gratitude project and book went through various iterations to become a good final product. Writing the book reminded me that personal and professional undertakings are never totally completed. Similarly, people are themselves *a work in progress*. The year of gratitude highlighted my own creative destruction and rebuilding. Having a great community and faith that things will work out makes any challenging season of life more bearable.

Humans are adaptable creatures. Like our ancient ancestors in the savannah, gratitude is a tool to navigate and defend social groups. Selfishly altruistic, genuine gratitude brings us together and elicits action. The fact that I experienced personal and community growth due to gratitude during a global pandemic, the most contested election in US history, racial tensions, and increased environmental concerns hopefully displays the immediate urgency to practice more gratitude. I wrote this book to let the world know that weekly, monthly, annual, or lifetime gratitude journeys are attainable. I hope the stories, observations, and frameworks of this book inspire new generations of gratitude practitioners. *Gratitude: a work in progress* is for those curious about consistent gratitude and brave enough to try.

Thank you!

END

acknowledgments

————

Throughout the book some names have been changed to protect the identity of individuals. Many of my "thank you" notes at the top of the chapters have been reconstructed. I did not start cataloging what I wrote until late into the process. The responses to my notes are mostly direct quotes, but again names may have been changed.

What better way to finish the book than with gratitude, acknowledgment, and reflection? Growing up, I had trouble reading. It still takes me a brutally long time to convert my mind's words into readable text, but that's another story. Thankfully, my parents signed me up for extra classes with our neighbor Mrs. Gregory in the first grade. Working with her, words started to make sense. My love for books and reading came from Mrs. Baker. In the first grade, she challenged the class. Students who read fifty books would get lunch with her. I made a pact with myself to be the first. Our library card became maxed out, and books were stacked high on the table counter, but after a few days, I was the first. Years later, to my surprise, when I wrote a list of accomplishments that I wanted to compete in my life—writing a book was high on the list. I believed the opportunity would come after years of experience. What did I have to offer as a young man?

Eric Koester, the Creator Institute's Founder and my professor, made me believe I had something to offer. What started as a book on entrepreneurship became a book about my gratitude journey. I didn't have to live my whole life before having a story to tell after all. The successful completion of this book is not only a reflection of me but the many wonderful people who have been part of the journey. Thirty-six recorded interviews, countless conversations, 365-plus "thank you" notes, existing research, and books helped me more clearly understand gratitude and tell a fraction of its stories. Undoubtedly, I will miss some names of people who have been part of this journey. Please forgive me if that is you. I will do my best to capture everyone.

Thank you, family. Mom, your unwavering love and support, and example of service set me up for a life of service. Dad, your guardrails and notes continue to guide me. Brooke, I doubt anyone understands me better. Thank you for being my best friend and constant confidant. Joby, you're alright. Thank you for being a supportive brother-in-law and husband to my sister. Daniel, our relationship continues to challenge me and push me to be a better person. Lisa, thanks for all your book recommendations! Christina, my love for you has only grown through this experience. No one else has witnessed the ups and downs of the process. Thank you for always being by my side. Sully, your wining, barking, and needs for pets helped me take the breaks I probably required. Blakely, Lane, Lucy, and Paisley, you are the joy of our family. Loretta, Pete,

Matt, and Ty, thank you for your support and interest. Bree, you came up big at the eleventh hour. The chapter on education would not be nearly as applicable without your input.

Gratitude note receivers. Thank you for being part of my gratitude project. I did not start writing "thank you" notes, knowing I would write a book. The relationships I have with you mean the world. It has been a blessing to receive your responses and interest throughout the experience.

My path to book publishing was through the Creator Institute and New Degree Press. Eric Koester and Laura Buckley, you started me off with the right foundation. Eric, your energy was contagious. That same energy spread belief and possibility. The Georgetown MBA experience would not have been nearly as good without you. (*still unsure whether you or your wife was the better teacher—haha.*) Laura, I hope the Magpies have finally succumbed to your constant affection. New Degree Press, the structure and support were extremely valuable. Camryn Privette, I hope I am not the most annoying author you guided over the finish line. Thank you for being flexible and supportive as my life changed and book writing became a lower priority.

The book truly started to take shape when Nicole Farrell kindly recommended reducing various chapters and restructuring the book. Nicole, you are a star and a wonderful friend. The book would not be nearly as exciting or good without your hand in editing. Wesley Stukenbroeker, even during summer camp, you were able to read the whole book and give me feedback within a day. Thank you for being a beta reader (*Shout out to Wes Notes— the next big thing!*) Sean Sweeney, you have seen the worst of my writing. Thanks for giving me another chance. Your serious recommendations and humorous comments made the editing process much more fun. I don't know what life would look like if my random freshman roommate wasn't you. Thanks, William & Mary.

Charles Shell, you challenged areas of my book that had yet to be challenged. Your comprehensive and long-term perspective shaped the book in ways I will forever be grateful. Professor Christine Porath, ever since I watched your TEDx Talk on "Mastering Civility," I have wanted to work with you. Thank you, under all your work and life pressure, for beta reading. Mrs. Peg Williams, it was surreal to have my fifth grade teacher beta reading my book. Thanks for making time! Thank you, Sugarcreek Schools, for helping me become a writer. Chris Murchison, interviewing you opened doors to relationships within the gratitude community. Thank you for that and beta reading! Christina, Mom, Brooke, and Daniel, you already got shoutouts, but thank you for beta reading!

Professor Amit Kumar, you were my first gratitude interview. Thank you for answering my email, giving me tons to think about, and remaining close throughout my journey. I find your research fascinating and can't wait to hear more about pro-social behaviors. Brian Doyle, your TEDx Talk was the first one I listened to on gratitude. Interviewing you was like interviewing a rock star. I found a kindred spirit during our conversation and have appreciated your friendship throughout. Darin Hollingsworth, talking to you was like talking to a long-lost friend. Thank you for exploring gratitude and my career. Our conversation opened the door to many valuable interviews and relationships. I look forward to our next call.

Though I could not quote or tell the story of every interview, the conversations gave me an immense understanding of gratitude and pertinent perspectives that shaped the book.

Thank you for a wonderful interview:

Adam Kuebler
Amit Kumar (Undervaluing Gratitude - Research)
Andrew Walker
Audrey Vanhoos
Blakely Myers
Brian Doyle (365 Days of Thank You - TED)
Charles Shell
Chris Murchison (Center for Positive Organizations - UofM)
Chris Palmore (Gratitudespace Radio)
Christine Porath (Mastering Civility)
Dan Brower
Dan Couladis
Darin Hollinsworth (Working Gratitude Podcast)
Dave Croall
Georgian Benta (The Gratitude Podcast)
Hannah Richards
Hrithik Bansal
Jo Englesson (Gratitude.com)
Joe Belsterling
Joe Staley
Keely Chase (Gratitude & Hallmark)
Kerry Wekelo (book)
Lynn Heidelbaugh (National Postal Museum)
Michael Lunchen

Mike Porath (CEO & Founder, The Mighty)

Sam Ducey

Samantha Gage

Kiran Thadhani (Co-Founder & Parnter, Santalum)

Kyle Gibson (Co-Founder & Partner, Santalum)

Rohan Shamapant

Scott Colby (Say it with Gratitude)

Shakeel Mohamaed

Simone G.

Stephanie Burns

Steve Forum (Gratitude Works)

Dr. Susan Smith (National Postal Musuem)

It is rather bizarre to ask family, friends, and acquaintances for money. To fund this book, that was what I had to do. The outreach turned out to be great opportunities to reconnect and share gratitude. The last fifty or so "thank yous" for my gratitude project came from this list of contributors. Thank you all for your support financially or through social media sharing! The book would not be possible without you:

Michael Brown	Rhys Tucker
Patrick Sweeney	Bruce Alexander
Sean Sweeney	Joe Staley
Prakhar Sharma	Jon Conway
Mac Williams	Stacey Truver
Dan Brower	Andrew Putz
Ricardo Rendon Cepeda	Janell Villasenor
Tyler Swope	Jeff Loeb
Eric Ottman	Michael Stockhausen
Charles Shell	Kord + Linda Basnight

Joellyn Pratt	Chris Vigilante - Vigilante Coffee
William Loyd	Bernardo Escudero Contag
Ryan Rogers	Carolyn Haller
Stacy Horner-Dunn	Kirby Horvitz
Janice Bowker	Lauren Rogers
Aaron Skonecki	Ellen Johnson
Nikhil Manojkumar	Dan Heffernan
Nick Smith	Julia Tvardovskaya
Joyce Kim	Dino Antoniou
Austen Brower	Eric Koester
Jay Ashe	Ann Canela
Shane Jason Wayne Meeker	Joshua Payton
Lynnewood Jeff Shafer II	Rebecca Silverstein
Patrick Conway	Melissa Alim
Gavin Oplinger	Srirama Josyula
Alexander Schmittlein	Chris Murchison
Quinn Marker	Brendan McNamara
Jeff Reid	Elizabeth B ONeirnr
Eric Young	Rodney Loges
Michael Biarnes	Joshua Thomas Miller
Adam Shepherd	Darin Hollingsworth
Muzna Abbas	Laura Buckley
Stacy Carnes	Will Maas
Dani Ross	Nichole Thomas
Chris Lynch	Mike O'Beirne
Michael Luchen	Nicole LaSota
Hanna Spears	Brandolon Barnett
Daniel Brower	Rohan Shamapant
Adam Kuebler	Brian Bok
Mitchell Batchelder	Tristan Schnader

Benjamin August	Susan Sando
Gopika Spaenle	James O'Beirne
Drew Hunt	Caitlyn McComb
Isaac Carp	Susan Ross
Adrian Vodislav	Macy Alexander
Jennifer Balios	Andrea Alvarez
Natalie Poston	Erin Hills
Libby Nicholson	Philip Basnight
Arianne Price	Wes Stukenbroeker
John-Mark Mocas	Pete Swope
Kevin Sullivan	Cynthia B Kenny
Alex Ross	Nicole & Victor Farrell
Matthew Pereira	Sarah Martin
Deepak Mishra	Stephanie Burns
Jamal Robinson	Kevin O'Connell
Kaitlyn Young	Christina R Swope
Jennie Cole	Austin Kaye
Miles Alexander	

Thank you, dear reader, for joining me on this journey—
stay mirthful.

Appendix

———

gratitude:

Seter, Bernie. "Thanksgiving And Thank You
Notes."*Northern Crossing*(blog).*Northern
Crossings Mercy,*November 24, 2018. https://www.
northerncrossingsmercy.org/thanksgiving-and-thank-
you-notes/.

Upholt, Boyce. "The Tumultuous History of the U.S. Postal
Service—and its Constant Fight for Survival."*National
Geographic,*May 18, 2020. https://www.
nationalgeographic.com/history/2020/05/tumultuous-
history-united-states-postal-service-constant-fight-
survival/.

a journey:

Algoe, B. Sara. "Find, Remind, and Bind: The Functions
of Gratitude in Everyday Relationships."*Social and
Personality Psychology Compass*6, no. 6 (2012). 455–469.
https://doi.org/10.1111/j.1751-9004.2012.00439.x.

Kumar, Amit, and Nicholas Epley. "Undervaluing Gratitude: Expressers Misunderstand the Consequences of Showing Appreciation."*Psychology Science*29, no 9 (June 27, 2018): 1423-1435. https://journals.sagepub.com/doi/10.1177/0956797618772506.

Metev, Denis. "How Much Time Do People Spend on Social Media? [63+ Facts to Like, Share and Comment]."*Review42*(blog), November 21, 2020. https://review42.com/how-much-time-do-people-spend-on-social-media/.

Ninivaggi, Frank J. "Loneliness: A New Epidemic in the USA."*Psychology Today*(blog), February 12, 2019. https://www.psychologytoday.com/us/blog/envy/201902/loneliness-new-epidemic-in-the-usa.

Renken, Elena. "Most Americans Are Lonely, And Our Workplace Culture May Not Be Helping."*NPR,*January 23, 2020. https://www.npr.org/sections/health-shots/2020/01/23/798676465/most-americans-are-lonely-and-our-workplace-culture-may-not-be-helping.

Simon-Thomas, Emiliana R., and Jeremy Adam Smith. "How Grateful are Americans?"*Greater Good Magazine*, January 10, 2013. https://greatergood.berkeley.edu/article/item/how_grateful_are_americans.

Williams, Lisa A. "Why Saying 'Thank You' Makes A Difference."*Lifehacker,*September 7, 2014. https://www.lifehacker.com.au/2014/09/why-saying-thank-you-makes-a-difference/.

a community:

Kralik, John.*365 Thank Yous: The Year a Simple Act of Daily Gratitude Changed My Life.*Read by John Kralik. London: Penguin eBooks, 2011. Audible audio ed., 5h 18m.

Jacobs, AJ. "A.J. Jacobs: My Journey to Thank All the People Responsible for my Morning Coffee." Filmed June 2018. TED Salon: Brightline Initiative video, 15.21. https://www.ted.com/talks/a_j_jacobs_my_journey_to_thank_all_the_people_responsible_for_my_morning_coffee.

TEDxYouth. "365 Days of Thank You: Brian Doyle." January 19, 2015. Video, 8:35. https://youtu.be/QNfAnkojhoE.

Tedx Talks. "365 Grateful Project | Hailey Bartholomew | TEDxQUT." September 2014. Video, 12:04. https://www.youtube.com/watch?v=zaufonUBjoQ.

a few learnings:

Algoe, B. Sara. "Find, Remind, and Bind: The Functions of Gratitude in Everyday Relationships."*Social and Personality Psychology Compass*6, no. 6 (2012).455–69 https://doi.org/10.1111/j.1751-9004.2012.00439.x.

Emmons, Dr. Robert A.*The Little Book of Gratitude: Create a Life of Happiness and Wellbeing by Giving Thanks.*London: Gaia Books, 2016.

Emmons, Robert. "Why Gratitude Is Good."*Greater Good Magazine,*November 16, 2010.https://greatergood.berkeley.edu/article/item/why_gratitude_is_good.

Jilani, Zaid, and Jeremy Adam Smith. "What Is the
True Cost of Polarization in America?"*Greater Good
Magazine,*March 4, 2019. https://greatergood.berkeley.
edu/article/item/how_grateful_are_americans.

Kaplan, Janice.*The Gratitude Diaries: How a Year Looking
on the Bright Side Can Transform You Life*. Read by Janice
Kaplan. London: Penguin Publishing Group, 2015. Audible
audio ed., 8h 12m.

Lambert, Nathaniel M, Margaret S. Clark, Jared Durtschi,
Frank D. Fincham, and Steven M. Graham. "Benefits of
Expressing Gratitude: Expressing Gratitude to a Partner
Changes One's View of the Relationship."*Psychological
Science*21, no. 4 (2010): 574-580 https://DOI:
10.1177/0956797610364003.

Pew Research Center. "Political Polarization in the
American Public." Internet & Research. Updated June
12, 2014. https://www.pewresearch.org/politics/
wp-content/uploads/sites/4/2017/10/10-05-2017-
Political-landscape-release-updt..pdf.

a science:

Emmons, Dr. Robert A.*The Little Book of Gratitude: Create a
Life of Happiness and Wellbeing by Giving Thanks.*London:
Gaia Books, 2016.

Fiske, Susan T., Amy J.C. Cuddy, and Peter Glick. "Universal
Dimensions of Social Cognition: Warmth and
Competence."*Trends in Cognitive Sciences,*2007.

Loewenstein C. George, Martin Weber, and Colin Camerer. "The Curse of Knowledge in Economic Settings: An Experimental Analysis."*Journal of Political Economy*97 (1989): 1232–1254.

Goldman, G. Jason. "Gratitude: Uniquely Human or Shared with Animals?"*The Thoughtful Animal* (blog). *Scientific American*, December 1, 2010. https://blogs. scientificamerican.com/thoughtful-animal/gratitude-uniquely-human-or-shared-with-animals/.

Kumar, Amit, and Nicholas Epley. "Undervaluing Gratitude: Expressers Misunderstand the Consequences of Showing Appreciation."*Psychology Science*29, no. 9 (June 27, 2018): 1423-1435. https://journals.sagepub.com/ doi/10.1177/0956797618772506.

The Table | Biola CCT."Gratitude Works!: The Science and Practice of Saying Thanks [Robert Emmons]." April 8, 2014. Video, 1:11:59. https://www.youtube.com/ watch?v=BF7xS_nPbZ0.

a mindset:

Morin, Amy. "7 Scientifically Proven Benefits Of Gratitude That Will Motivate You To Give Thanks Year-Round."*Forbes,*November 23, 2014. https://www.forbes. com/sites/amymorin/2014/11/23/7-scientifically-proven-benefits-of-gratitude-that-will-motivate-you-to-give-thanks-year-round.

TEDxPugetSound. "Start with Why -- How Great Leaders Inspire Action | Simon Sinek | TEDxPugetSound."

September 29, 2009. Video, 18:01. https://www.youtube.
com/watch?v=u4ZoJKF_VuA.

a recognition:

Chalabi, Mona. "How Many People Can You
Remember?"*FiveThirtyEight,*September 23, 2015. https://
fivethirtyeight.com/features/how-many-people-can-
you-remember/.

Gallup. "CliftonStrengths Explains How You Are Uniquely
Powerful." Accessed January 15, 2021. https://www.
gallup.com/cliftonstrengths/en/252137/home.aspx.

Gallup. "Talent X Investment = Strength." Accessed January
15, 2021. https://www.gallup.com/cliftonstrengths/
en/253790/science-of-cliftonstrengths.aspx.

Jo Englesson. "Bio | Jo Englesson." Jo Englesson Bio.
Accessed on February 23, 2021. https://www.
joenglesson.com/bio.

Tedx Talks. "365 Grateful Project | Hailey Bartholomew |
TEDxQUT." September 2014. Video, 12:04. https://www.
youtube.com/watch?v=zaufonUBjoQ.

an expression:

Kralik, John.*365 Thank Yous: The Year a Simple Act of Daily
Gratitude Changed My Life.*Read by John Kralik. London:
Penguin eBooks, 2011. Audible audio ed., 5h 18m.

Pols, Lucas. "Leadership: The Importance Of Removing
    Barriers Facing Your Employees."*Forbes,*January
    2, 2019. https://www.forbes.com/sites/
    forbeslacouncil/2019/01/02/leadership-the-importance-
    of-removing-barriers-facing-your-employees/.

BrainyQuotes. "Abraham Lincoln Quotes." Last modified
    2021. Accessed on February 21, 2021. https://www.
    brainyquote.com/quotes/abraham_lincoln_109275.

an opportunity:

Altman, Jack. "How Much Does Employee Turnover Really
    Cost?"*HuffPost,*January, 18 2017. https://www.huffpost.
    com/entry/how-much-does-employee-turnover-really-
    cost_b_587fbaf9e4b0474ad4874fb7.

CMX. "3 Million Registered Users. Zero Marketing Dollars
    | Mike Porath." October 7, 2019. Video, 22:04. https://
    youtu.be/MidSwTQAoGM.

Crunchbase. "Gregory Kenny - Member of Board of
    Directors @ AK Steel." Accessed on October 10, 2020.
    https://www.crunchbase.com/person/gregory-b-kenny.

Fountain, Susan, Linda Lantieri, Melody Baker, and Caroline
    Zayas King. "Nurturing Gratitude From the Inside Out:
    30 Activities for Grades K-8." Greater Good Science
    Center,2017. https://ggsc.berkeley.edu/who_we_serve/
    educators/educator_resources/gratitude_curricula.

Froh, Jeffrey and Giacomo Bono. "How to Foster Gratitude
    in Schools."*Greater Good Magazine,*November 9, 2012.

https://greatergood.berkeley.edu/article/item/how_to_
foster_gratitude_in_schools.

Greater Good Science Center. "Gratitude Curricula | Greater
Good Science Center." Gratitude Curricula. Last Updated
October 11, 2020. Accessed on October 12, 2020. https://
ggsc.berkeley.edu/who_we_serve/educators/educator_
resources/gratitude_curricula.

Greater Good Science Center. "How Can We Cultivate
Gratitude in Schools?" September 29, 2014. Video, 17:19.
https://youtu.be/Qhqy_A9G4_M.

Kelly, Jack. "More Than Half Of U.S. Workers Are Unhappy
In Their Jobs: Here's Why And What Needs To Be Done
Now." *Forbes,* October 25, 2019. https://www.forbes.
com/sites/jackkelly/2019/10/25/more-than-half-of-
us-workers-are-unhappy-in-their-jobs-heres-why-and-
what-needs-to-be-done-now/?sh=4592dd032024.

Kohll, Alan. "What Employees Really Want At
Work." *Forbes,* July 10, 2018. https://www.forbes.com/
sites/alankohll/2018/07/10/what-employees-really-
want-at-work/?sh=133589405ad3.

The Mighty. "Who We Are | The Mighty." Accessed on
January 21, 2021. https://themighty.com/who-we-are/.

a work in progress

Ducharme, Jamie. "COVID-19 Is Making America's
Loneliness Epidemic Even Worse." *Time,* May 8, 2020.
https://time.com/5833681/loneliness-covid-19/.

Emmons, Dr. Robert A.*The Little Book of Gratitude: Create a Life of Happiness and Wellbeing by Giving Thanks.*London: Gaia Books, 2016.

Grant, Adam. "Give and Take: A Revolutionary Approach to Success." Read by Adam Grant. London: Penguin Audio, 2019. Audible audio ed., 6h 56m.

Kaplan, Janice. "The Gratitude Diaries: How a Year Looking on the Bright Side Can Transform Your Life." Read by Janice Kaplan. London: Penguin Audi, 2015. Audible audio ed., 8h 12m.

Oxford Languages Online. s.v. "altruism." Accessed on January 21, 2021. https://www.google.com/search?q=definition+of+altruism&rlz=1C5CHFA_enU-S857US858&oq=definition+of+altruism&aqs=-chrome..69i57j0l6j0i22i30l3.11374j1j4&sourceid=-chrome&ie=UTF-8.

Made in the USA
Middletown, DE
29 June 2021

43340702R00084